Women Today

Making a Difference

A COLLECTION OF TRUE STORIES

Compiled By Dorothy K. Ederer

Sr. Dorothy Ederer :)

Acknowledgements

There are no words to express my gratitude to Christopher W. Tremblay for the exquisite job he continues to do on my book covers.

Thanks to Melissa Coll-Smith for her excellent job of editing.

Thank you to the women who shared their stories from their hearts.

Table of Contents

Introduction

Today, it is hard to find role models for our young women that they can relate to. There definitely is not a shortage of inspiring women who have done amazing things.

In this book, I am featuring **women who have made a difference**. They found their passion and were courageous enough for it to become a reality.

I hope you are inspired to find your passion, live it, but don't compromise your morals and values!

Women Today

They love without question.
They're strong in their
convictions.
They are beautiful.
They are passionate.
They are generous.
They are creative.
They are committed.
They are prayerful.
dke

6

Follow Your Vision
Follow Your Dream

Even the most attractive people have to deal with some insecurities related to their appearance. The face is what people notice first. This is why the condition of our skin is incredibly important to our confidence for any time in our life.

Growing up in Russia, I struggled with an oily and acne-prone complexion and it was difficult to find solutions while avoiding antibiotics or other topical medications. Probiotics and Compresses from herbal extracts of calendula, burdock root, and celandine helped me to achieve the level of skin balance that I was satisfied with. Being able to improve my skin holistically was an incredible relief and gave me inspiration to learn more about herbs and phytotherapy.

Sometimes, I would experience premonitions seeing myself in a very cozy room filled with botanical aromas while giving a face treatment to a woman. She was sharing with me her concerns and dreams and I was trying my best to make her look and feel better by listening and mixing unique botanical potions for her skin. I could not exactly understand what this vision meant, because I definitely did not want to become a conventional doctor or pharmacist.

At the age of 16, I received a couple of facials from one of the salons in Moscow. The facials consisted of only steaming, extractions, massage, and applications of masks and lotions.

A few years later, I ended up receiving a teaching degree and worked at a school and publishing house. At the same time, I was continuously studying chemistry, herbalism, and esthetics and learning how to make natural creams and homeopathic ointments.

In 1991, I arrived in the United States with my husband Igor and our baby boy, Yuri. Igor is a very talented violinist and professor of music at Western Michigan University. For several years, after I improved my English and had received my esthetician license. I worked as an esthetician and formulator for a spa and for a plastic surgeon. I did not feel completely satisfied because I continuously had flashing memories of my vision of that cozy treatment room filled with healing energy and special botanical extracts and potions. I decided to make this vision a reality.

In 1998 I opened my first spa and finally launched my own skin care line. I did this all by myself, giving facials throughout the day, formulating and making organic, edible skin care products in the evenings and weekends. My son, Yuri was only seven years old at that time.

Sometimes I had to take him to work, where he would interact with clients and watch me work in the lab. I even took him to some ingredient trade shows or cosmeceutical summits for formulators. I still feel guilty for working very long hours when Yuri was at such an impressionable age. When you hear a business owner saying that they work twenty-four-seven, it is the absolute truth. Therefore, I believe you should only start your own business if you cannot imagine your life without it.

Yuri became fascinated with formulating natural skin care products and decided to make it his career. Now, he is 27 years old and we create products together. I cannot even imagine how I would be able to keep up with production without him.

In this country, twenty years ago, the holistic approach to beauty was not a popular trend. It was difficult to source clean, botanical ingredients. I ended up purchasing most of my ingredients from overseas. I had to explain to my clients why I was offering them natural enzymes in place of chemical peels, and why ingredients extracted from organic plants work better for their skin.

My clients were starting to share and support the holistic approach by seeing great results on their faces after just the first appointment and shortly after using the products. This is why my spa got popular and I started to hire and train people. Other salon owners, doctors and estheticians were contacting me regularly asking me to train them on my techniques. They also wanted to carry my product line. At that time, I realized that there is a big need for professional education in Holistic Skin Care.

In 2007, I started the Association of Holistic Skin Care Practitioners. The AHSCP provides professional education on noninvasive methods and natural ingredients for corrective, anti-aging and anti-inflammatory skin care treatments. We know that beauty is more than skin deep and that a person is much more than a physical body. By taking a holistic approach to our health and lives, we can take better care of ourselves and help to create a more harmonious life for the entire world: practicing holistic skin care is a large part of making this happen.

For many years, I have appeared on Elina Skin Cuisine TV segments showing natural beauty recipes on different morning shows and I see how people have become more and more responsive to my segments over the years.

It makes me happy to see that more people are realizing that beauty products that they apply to their skin everyday may end up in their blood-stream. The "green" movement is coming to all aspects of our lives such as clean food, organic clothing, gardening or landscaping, skincare and makeup. That is why they are seeking clean food grade ingredients. I believe I was and still am playing a role during this Green movement and that makes me very happy and proud.

During this 20-year journey I have met many wonderful friends and professionals who work with my product line all around the country. I am grateful for the surrounding love and support at Elina Organics, for my employees who I have worked with for many years.

I received an industry recognition and several awards for my formulations, as an esthetician and educator. My only hope is that our holistic approach to life will continue to inspire others to bring more beauty, health, peace, and harmony to our entire planet.

Elina's work continues to inspire others and she is known around the world for her work in skin care. She has won numerous awards. Here are a few:

+ 2012: Chicago Magazine Voted Elina Organics Best Facial in Chicago 2012.

+2018: A List Awards "Recognizing Excellence" by Dermascope Magazine. Elina was voted as one of the A LIST Estheticians for 2018 "The Holistic Professional"

+For that same feature we also won "LEADING LINES" for the Elina Organics Line and "BREAKING THE MOLD" for her edible grade aesthetics.

+Dermascope Voted Amethyst Polish as Best Exfoliator of the year for 2018

+CS Magazine voted Elina Organics as the Best Faial for Glowing Skin in Chicago 2019

+Chicago Magazine Voted Elina Organics Best Skin Care Spas to Banish Dry Skin 2019

+Dermascope voted Ambra Lift Elixir as best Moisturizer of the year for 2019.

Questions to Ponder

When was the last time you treated yourself to a facial?

Our skin care products are organic. They are eatable. Can you consume your skin care products?

Author
Elina Fedotova and Igor Fedotov and their son Yuri
Elina Organics
Kalamazoo, Michigan and Chicago, Illinois

"For beautiful eyes,
look for the
good in others;
for beautiful lips,
speak only words of
kindness."
Audrey Hepburn

A Revolution of Love

After almost 40 years of ministry to young women, what I've found they most often struggle to know and believe is expressed by three simple words: *"Who am I?"* My own quest to answer this question began as a young girl (an identical twin), was tested through family tragedy, distorted by desperate choices, and finally redeemed by God's love.

My Jewish identity began at birth and was formed by my very Jewish grandparents, the practice of Jewish customs and the study of the Torah and culminated in my Bat Mitzvah at age thirteen. My world was predominantly Jewish, and as a child I thought everyone in the world was Jewish!

One snowy night in December, halfway through my sophomore year in high school, my 18-year-old brother was killed suddenly in a violent car accident. My faith, expressed primarily through customs and traditions, now at best seemed shallow, if not empty.

My confusion, grief, and anger sparked extensive questions about the existence of God, the meaning of life, and my own purpose. I struggled to make sense of this painful tragedy, and in the absence of significant answers I turned to partying, sexual promiscuity, and academic achievements.

Eager to leave home, I enrolled at The University of Michigan and my exposure to different beliefs and people was widened. My first roommate and other girls in my dorm not only called themselves Christians, but also claimed to know their God in a personal way. I didn't know anything about Jesus or their religion, but I did know their beliefs were off-limits to me, a Jew.

One day while writing a paper, I needed to borrow one of my friend's Christian Bible. I was met by several surprises. Not only did her Bible contain the Jewish Scriptures, but she read it, as evidenced by her underlining and comments in the margins. I couldn't decipher Paul's letter to the Romans (the text for my assignment), but it was clear to me that these ancient words spoken to my friend. How could a book filled with stories and myths be alive?

Later that semester, that same friend invited me to watch a movie in the dorm lounge. If I had known it was called *Jesus of Nazareth*, I never would have gone. But as I watched, something both alarming and intriguing became evident—Jesus was a Jew, a good Jew! In one scene, he arrived in Bethany and was met by a weeping woman named Mary, who exclaimed, "Lord, if only you had been here, my brother would not have died." I too, had uttered those same words many times to a seemingly distant, unknowable God. Absorbed in the story, I followed Jesus to the tomb of Lazarus—four days buried—and watched as he brought him back from the dead. "What if," I thought, "death is not the final answer?" Unable to sleep, I borrowed that same Bible and for the first time, I read all four Gospels. Late that night I spoke to a God I wasn't even sure existed. "God if you are real, if Jesus is the Messiah, show me and give me the faith to believe."

That prayer and Bible became my constant companions over the next nine months as I examined the claims of Christ, studied Messianic prophecies, and wrestled with the cost of discipleship. One night in early December of my sophomore year of college, I had a dream. I was standing at the end of a long, dark hallway, and a voice called out to me: "Who do you say I am?" Finally, as the question was posed for the third time, the darkness lifted, and I saw Jesus standing before me. I awoke from the dream knowing I had made an intellectual assent to the truth about Jesus, but I lacked the faith conviction to make this reality my own and to risk losing my family.

One night a week later, I was sitting on my bed in my dorm room reciting the now familiar prayer: "God, show me who you are and give me the faith to believe." As I reflected on all the ways I had disobeyed God's commands and failed to acknowledge Him, suddenly the room seemed to fill with a light and presence. I knew in some inexplicable way that God was there with me in the person of Jesus, who extended his hand as if offering me a gift. I understood it was what I had asked for—the gift of faith. And despite all the years of never knowing him, in my grief, questioning, and unbelief, I knew it was all true. Jesus was the Messiah, sent to rescue and restore me to a relationship with my heavenly Father.

I began a time of spiritual growth and trans-formation and I wanted to share His love with everyone I met! Perhaps it was the pain of my own teenage years that stirred in me a conviction and passion to help young women also find their true identity in Christ.

My ministry to young women grew from sharing my story on coffee dates in campus ministry. Newly married, I had a dream to create and direct a week-long Christian camp for junior high girls—an environment where young girls could personally encounter the love of God through prayer, music, friendships, staff, and fun activities. That dream became a reality 33 years later.

Pine Hills Girls Camp is not just a week-long event, but a powerful culture of love, in which almost 300 young women are empowered and equipped to live and share their faith.

As the world becomes increasingly challenging and even hostile to Christianity, it became clear to me that we needed to extend this beautiful mission beyond the confines of camp or a singular event and begin a movement for high school girls. In August of 2013, during the closing night of another powerful camp season, the Lord spoke these words to me clearly:

"If each one of these young women, filled with the love of God and one another, takes that love out into the world, and touches one life, we can start a Revolution."

Five years ago, we launched Be Love Revolution whose mission is three-fold:

- **Be His** - To help young women know the personal and transformative love of Jesus.
- **Be Free** - To radically change young women's self-perception and help them live freely and confidently.
- **Be Love** - To teach and empower young women to be God's love in the world today.

Today we have more than 100 teenage girls who meet weekly for our local *Be Loved* events, and we have chapters beginning in the U.S. and Canada. This all-girl environment gives them the opportunity to learn how to be *for* one another, rather than adversaries and enemies, and they develop life-long bonds of friendship, support, and sisterhood.

We also lead high school, junior high and parish retreats, small groups and weekly Bible studies; we conduct annual mission trips to the garbage dump in Mexico City, personally mentor and disciple young women, and provide support to parents. We now have a paid staff of five, a college intern, and many volunteers. We are raising up leaders and empowering hundreds of young women to confidently live their faith and use their gifts and talents to bring God's love to those around them.

The needs around us are immense, yet each young revolutionary of love, supported by her sisters in Christ, and inspired the words and example of our patron saint Mother Teresa, is striving to change the world—one day and one person at a time—by "doing small things with great love."

Questions to Ponder

How have you experienced God breaking into your own life to reveal His love to you?

In what ways is He calling you to share the reality of His love with those around you?

Author
Debbie Herbeck and her husband Peter
Debbie is an author and speaker, and the
Executive Director of Pine Hills Girls Camp and the
Founder and Director of Be Love Revolution.
Ann Arbor, Michigan

"Having a sister is like having a best friend you can't get rid of. You know whatever you do, they'll still be there."

Amy Li

Kindness is Contagious

Seven years ago, Nicole's life looked perfect, at least in photos. She had a wonderful husband, three beautiful children, her Broadcast Journalism degree from the University of Wisconsin, 10 years of experience as a news anchor and enough beauty to earn a Miss Wisconsin title. But Nicole was depressed and on the edge of becoming what anyone would call an alcoholic...she was a drinker, a smoker, an overeater, and angry at her husband most of the time. She says life felt passionless and pointless.

She was called by the publisher of her local newspaper and asked to write a column. She was interested in the idea but couldn't figure out anything she wanted to write about every week. Politics, cooking and parenting all ran through her head, but she quickly talked herself out of each one as she realized she really couldn't be considered an expert on any of these topics.

Then one day, in Fargo, North Dakota, she went to the public swimming pool with her three small children and met a teenage girl in a shiny gold bikini. It turns out "Gold Bikini Girl" was a young mom, and even without a support system and adequate resources, she somehow seemed joyful and engaged in her daughter's life, something Nicole immediately admired.

When they were getting ready to leave the pool (Nicole into her brand-new minivan and Gold Bikini Girl into a clunker of a vehicle), Nicole heard a little voice in her head say, "Give her some money." She fumbled through her purse and grabbed all that she had - three $20 bills- and handed it to the girl while mumbling something about being inspired by their short visit. The exchange was awkward but brought tears to the eyes of the girl in the gold bikini.

Nicole walked away with a high unlike anything she had ever felt before. It was better than any self-medicating she had tried to do in the past through drinking, smoking, shopping or eating. In that moment, Gold Bikini Girl taught Nicole a secret that changed her life:

Kindness isn't about them, it's about you. The life you transform with kindness is your own.

Nicole knew if everyone knew what that high felt like, they would all want to try it and kindness would be contagious. That became the title of Nicole's weekly newspaper column and first book: *Kindness is Contagious.*

Within one year of being intentional about kindness, Nicole quit smoking and drinking, lost 30 pounds, and re-fell in love with her husband. Nicole didn't stop there - she was now on a mission to tell the world about Kindness. As a former news anchor and former Miss Wisconsin, she used this experience to speak about Kindness to schools, hospitals, churches, and other organizations. Her email inbox was piling up with stories that readers were submitting, and she wrote her first book *Kindness is Contagious* in November 2016. Her email continued to explode with stories of kindness from readers and in September 2018, she launched her second book titled *Kindness is Courageous.*

As a Kindness Advocate, Nicole is now on a mission to spread kindness through the world and inspire those around her to "try it" and think intentionally about ways to be kind to others. Her message is captivating and is spoken from the heart.

After hearing her speak, September 2017, three women approached Nicole to ask if they could support her in her efforts to spread the message of kindness. So, Nicole created a "kindness team" to help with booking speaking engagements, media appearances and book signings as her business was growing.

Her favorite audience to speak to are those in the caregiving fields who show kindness every day. She teaches that kindness is powerful and it has teeth. It's not just a fluffy feel good term. She also teaches her audience that the key to adding more kindness in our lives is perspective.

We can go to a restaurant and notice that the server is a little crabby and the soup is a little cold and the kitchen put tomatoes on our sandwich OR we can go to that restaurant and notice they gave us a lovely seat right by the window, and we can be delighted that we have an hour to spend with someone we care about, and we can leave feeling grateful that we got to eat dinner and didn't have to wash any dishes. It's all a matter of perspective.

We get bombarded by the bad news, while truly there is so much goodness in this world going on each day. But we can miss it if we're not tuned in and trained to look for it.

Here is Nicole's favorite kindness story: There was a man driving through a little strip mall that happened to have a drive-thru coffee shop. The man was driving from one direction when he encountered a woman in a car coming from the other direction. They made eye contact through the windshield, but it wasn't a friendly eye contact. The woman's eyes seemed to say, "Don't even think of getting your coffee before me."

The woman then floored it and cut the man off as she pulled into the drive-thru. Now the funny thing is, the man wasn't even going to the drive-thru, he was simply driving through the parking lot. But at that moment, he decided to park and go into the coffee shop. He told the barista he wanted to pay for whatever that woman was ordering from the drive-thru.

Astounded, Nicole asked him why he did that. He said, "I could have gone to work and complained about how terrible people are. People would have agreed with me and shared their own stories. The entire day would have gone negative. But by taking five minutes to buy her coffee, instead, I got to walk around all day thinking about how clever I am!"

Nicole is a remarkable and inspiring woman. Not only did she experience the power of kindness and turned her own life around, she is now on a mission to tell the world about the impact kindness can have to truly make this a better place for all of us to live.

"Kindness is the language which the deaf can hear and the blind can see."

Mark Twain

Question to Ponder

What is one act of kindness you remember someone doing for you?

Author

Nicole Philips and her husband Saul have three children. She is a Kindness Champion who has been called upon to share her ideas on the Hallmark Channel, in *Reader's Digest*, through her weekly Kindness Podcast, and in a weekly newspaper column (Kindness is Contagious) which runs in North Dakota and Minnesota as well as speaking opportunities throughout the nation. Athens, Ohio

Visit BraveandKind.net for more information.

Changing Lives
One Voice at a Time

I started as a singer with a love to sing and a desire to be a worship leader

Over the past 16 years, I had a lot of time to think, be introspective and had to ask myself hard questions. Both of my parents have been heavily involved with ministry and giving back to others. After a long time of doing nothing, being a work from home Mom and sitting on my gifts, I started to think what I had to give back. I wanted to give back to single parents and children who lacked confidence and strong support systems. I thought if only I had the confidence and support to pursue my dreams, I might not have found myself in the situation I did. What if I could stop other children and parents from going through what I had?

I started the project as a nonprofit effort with the end goal to own a retreat center where single mothers could come live for a year, with child care, seed money for businesses, nutrition and financial counseling, estate planning, and everything they need to become self-sustaining individuals.

I traveled the country learning all I could to sustain the vision, but when I returned home, many began to talk me out of my dream and ask what I would do for a revenue source. So, like Moses, I thought to myself, "What do I have in my hands?" I had my music and motivation. So, I went after my trademark, "Live Your Song," and wanted to teach people that like music, they can take the highs and lows of life, the pauses and rests, the rhythms and riffs and create a beautiful anthem that could last for generations to come. Thus, in my pursuit to leave a legacy, two products were born.

Melody's Song and the City of the Voice Snatchers

In the book, Melody lives in a city that powered by music. Every 30 days someone writes the town song to power the city for 30 days. Melody knows one day her song will be chosen, but every time she goes to sing, something crazy happens. She opens her mouth to sing and frogs come out. Another time she opens her mouth to sing and her feet run backwards the other direction. The kids are always making fun of her, but her mother keeps telling her she's a special little girl.

One day at school, they announce a talent show where whoever wins gets to power the city for 30 days. Melody just knows this is her chance. She excitedly tells her mother who begs her not to do it. What do you think Melody does? She auditions, but when she opens her mouth to sing, nothing comes out. Instead, she opens her mouth to sing and several butterflies come out with a huge hand that scratches the chalkboard from top to bottom. The kids laugh and make fun of her. Melody is devastated, and she says she will never sing again. That's when her Mother tells her the secret. When she was born it was foretold that she would be the girl with the golden voice. That's when the voice snatchers started attacking the city kidnapping the singers to power their own dark city. To protect her, her mother took her voice and had it sealed away.

I won't tell you the ending, but it's a powerful story about self-love, self-awareness, self-confidence and self-identity. Children love the story and in book two, she learns more about the power of her voice travels to Sound Kingdom where she is introduced to her sidekicks the "Sound Catchers." They are a jazz quartet band. She is tasked with traveling back to Dark Alley to take on the Chief Voice Snatcher and help set the other kidnapped voices free. It teaches the power of humility, checking your ego, collaboration and teamwork.

Voiceprint: How to find your voice, live your song, and unleash purpose

Voiceprint is a powerful leadership and personal development book that shares personal triumphs/failures and teaches people how to tap into their unique voiceprint, so they can start living their song. In the book, I discuss how Google, Alexa and Siri are catching on to the power of the voice, but many people are missing it. I also talk about how there are two laws that govern the universe, the "law of the speed of light" and the "law of the speed of sound."

I share my equation that Voice + Vision = Velocity and the tools that helped change my life (vision boards and affirmations). I also talk about the power of frequencies and that sometimes when we are changing our life or tapping into our true voiceprint, we need to change our frequencies.
I share with the reader tools I created: A Voice Map Canvas, Voiceprint Workbook and Guide, and Voiceprint Journal. I also provide follow up coaching and share that most people fall into four categories: Voice Search, Voice Recognition, Voice Identification and Voice Activation. The goal of the book and tools is to get everyone into Voice Activation.

To date, I have served approximately 400 children through my after school and summer programs that teaches children how to find their voice, unlock their passion, identify the voice snatchers in their lives and use music/other creative strategies to defeat them.

Here is a list of my songs:

"I Belong To You," "Tender Mercy," "I Never Knew," "Can't Nobody" — all found on youtube.com.

Melody's Song is a 10-book series that combines music and motivation to teach children how to find their voice, unlock it, pursue their passion and identify/ defeat the potential Voice Snatchers in their lives.

Here are the first books in the series (you can find each at melodyssong.com:

- Melody's Song and the City of the Voice Snatchers (Book 1)
- Melody's Song and the Adventure of the Sound Catchers (Book 2)
- Melody's Songbook of Freedom: A Look Back at The Songs That Helped Rewrite African American Black History (Special Edition)

The goal of the books and afterschool program: The story teaches and empowers children with self-confidence, perseverance, self-awareness, self-love, self-identity, self-esteem, self-fulfillment, goal-directed behavior, social-awareness, and decision making.

Question to Ponder

What will you do with what's in your hands?

Ponder this quote:

"…No two people on earth are alike, and it's got to be that way in music, or it isn't music."

Billy Holiday

Author
Lonna Hardin is a singer, author, consultant and founder of melodyssong.com and iamlonna.com.
liveyoursong@iamlonna.com
Kalamazoo, Michigan

A Classroom Inside the Walls

Beth Deacon is a high school mathematics teacher that has been changing lives of students, both teen and adult aged, for over twenty-five years. Although her most recent work is in the public-school setting, she found a new appreciation for life after working in the walls of a maximum-security prison. As she gifted these men with knowledge, confidence, kindness, respect, and value; they gifted her with a new set of eyes. Let's learn, as she writes of how mutual respect, hard work, and life lessons helped these men find success and then what inspired her to go back to the public-school setting.

"I remember my first day of work at the prison. I was not nervous, which most didn't understand. My mindset was very positive as I knew; mutual respect, my love for teaching and desire to help others would once again make for a successful experience. As I walked into the classroom, I noticed the men watched every move I made and wondered why I was there. What was my motive? Most had little to no support from family and friends; why would they expect any different from me? What the offenders didn't understand is that I was now their teacher and I would be the motivation that changed their lives. In their minds, my motivation was a paycheck. The men misjudged me. This was one of the first lessons about life they encountered through my teaching.

The school was functioning as an independent study program. I sat next to the first student that wanted help. He was struggling to solve a math problem. After we tackled the problem together, he looked at me and said, "You aren't scared. You aren't even nervous. Why?" I responded, "I am not here to judge you. I believe everyone can be successful with hard work. I don't care why you are here, I only care what you do from this point on." He looked at me and smiled. I knew at that moment he would graduate; pass his test. He graduated and now lives in the free world.

What drives me is others' successes. I noticed quickly that students were content sitting at computers, listening to music, and making no progress. These men were paid to attend school and money was their motivation to be present each day. They weren't expecting to graduate which was unacceptable to me. A change needed to be made.

The biggest obstacle for many was passing the math GED test. Some had been in school for years with no success. Math is my love and so I decided we would conquer this fear early on. I found a small whiteboard and began teaching. I would not allow these men to feel self-pity. We were moving forward and not looking back. We worked hard every day. I didn't want to hear can't in class. If the prison was on restricted move, I went to the mens' cells to make sure they continued working. We had a test to prepare for and they were going to be successful.

On test day, all six men came to class looking very nervous and tired. I said to them, "I believe in you. If I didn't think you were ready to test, you wouldn't be testing. Believe in yourselves, you can do it." The first student came out with a smile on his face. He looked at me with tears and I knew he had passed. He said he not only passed for his mother but for me. He sat in disbelief with tears coming down his face, hoping his classmates would be successful also.

That day every one of the students came out with a smile, tears of joy, and more confidence than ever. I shed a few tears myself as I watched them, through the window, walking back to their units with their heads held high and smiles on their faces; excited to call home with their incredible news.

They now not only believed in themselves, but they believed in me. They knew I would not allow them to give up. The success of these students in math class, peaked more interest as others started to attend school. When I began teaching at the prison there were approximately 12 students. When I left three years later there were 48 and many graduates.

As school became traditional, I required more; it was time to begin teaching them about life. Students were assigned seats next to people they did not associate with outside of school. They learned another life lesson that was more valuable than I even imagined. At one of the graduation ceremonies, a graduate walked over to me and shook my hand. He said that I taught him more than I would ever understand. He smiled and said, "I use to be racist, thank you."

We learned, failed, and succeeded together. I instilled in them that our world is precious because we are all unique. Some were good readers; others found an interest in history while some enjoyed computations. We took advantage of each other's strengths and were successful because of it. I didn't judge them and they didn't judge each other. The men started giving compliments to classmates. "Failure makes us stronger," became our motto.

School became the safe zone as no one was judged.

Teaching became even more enjoyable for me as the men became comfortable and confident in school. Many started reading out loud in class. You may not think this is a big deal, but to these men, many of which were reading at low levels, it was huge. To be in prison and show your weaknesses to others, that just doesn't happen.

The school officer, who had worked at the prison for over 20 years, came to me one day and asked me to go for a walk down the hall with him. He took me into the card room where one of my students was studying intensely. The officer looked at me and said he had never seen that in all the years he worked in the prison. He said, "These men respect you. They want to prove to you they can accomplish their goals to graduate. You are making a huge difference here. Be proud of what you are accomplishing". As we walked down the hall, he quietly once again shook his head and said, "I have never seen anything like this before."

I was honored to be the state "Correctional Teacher of the Year" for 2016-2017. The most meaningful part of this award was the excitement my students portrayed when they learned of it. Listening to the men speak in such high regards of me, truly showed I was making a difference. I remember one graduate standing at the podium, looked over at me and said, "You never judged us, you believed in us. You are the true definition of a teacher."

If I did not gain the respect of these men, they would not learn. I had to hold them accountable, push them, and teach them the importance of teamwork. Although most of these men had life sentences, I did not fear them as I viewed them as my students. I didn't sugar coat anything as I held them to high standards. Most never had anyone that respected or believed in them. Once they saw that I cared, they wanted to be successful. They wanted to make me proud.

I remember my last day at the prison. Some men cried as they didn't want me to leave. They felt they needed me to be successful. They asked me to open my heart to all the kids in need and not allow them to end up in prison. I was so proud that day. These men learned more than math, science, writing and social studies, they learned to appreciate, respect and care about others. I have a new appreciation for life and I thank the students I worked with at the prison.

To be a woman and teach in a men's prison was challenging. Not all these men acted civilized.

I endured many rude comments, received unwanted stares, and taught murderers, rapists and other convicted felons. And although I thought of them as students, I was always cognizant of my environment. I was questioned many times in the public as to why I would help these offenders. What no one seemed to understand is that these men were paying for their transgressions. I was hired to teach and my nonjudgmental attitude and respect towards these men changed them in ways no one will understand. With an education, some will find success in the free world, while others will live their lives in prison mentoring those that will be given a second chance.

When I decided to continue my teaching career in the public-school setting, I wanted to go where the need was the greatest. The school I chose, is over 60% poverty rate and is ranked in the bottom 19% of schools in the state. But my students will succeed because I won't give up on them.

Helping others is where I find my true happiness. Having a positive role, in opening kids' minds to this amazing world, is priceless. I strive to show kids they define who they are and who they will become. I am proud to call myself a teacher.

Question to Ponder

What can be done to change a person's future?

Author
Beth Deacon
Secondary Mathematics Teacher
25 years' experience in teaching
Keokuk High School, Keokuk, Iowa
Fort Madison, Iowa

"God used beautiful

mathematics in

creating the world."

Paul Dirac

Don't Waste a Good Crisis

I was blindsided. Here I was, a thirty-year old wife and mother of two young-children, ages four and two, working as a licensed assistant to an advisor in the financial industry. I was taking care of his clients at work and taking care of my family at home. Then one day, a knock came on the door of that home, and two men in black suits with dark glasses, just like you see in the movies, were standing on my porch. They flashed their badges and asked to come in. They were from the IRS and they were investigating my boss for tax fraud—Blindsided.

When I went back to work the next day, I went straight to his office, closed the door and told him to level with me. We had been working together for ten years. He was a mentor, a friend and someone I trusted and looked up to. He was honest—well, mostly honest—and said he made a mistake. He told me that what he had done did not affect our clients or our business, but he was in trouble. A few days later, he called a meeting with me and the other assistant and asked us to step forward and become the lead advisors of his practice. He asked this so that we could keep the business going and he would have something to come back to, should he go to jail. Honestly, I would come to see later that he was being very selfish and only thinking of himself. I have to admit, I was a bit selfish too when I first said yes. I had a very good job that I loved, I enjoyed the clients with whom I worked, and most of all, I was able to have flexible hours and be the kind of mom I always dreamed of being. Here he was, telling me I may lose it all. And worst of all, I realized, our clients would be hurt and spread to the wind, at no fault of their own, being forced to choose a stranger as their advisor, if I said no. Not only would their trust be broken, but now their financial future and security could be in danger. I knew I couldn't let that happen. So, I stepped up and stepped forward, taking on the responsibility to care for these clients as my own, and walking with them through this transition. We had to form a new firm, and we needed to have a conversation with each and every one of them, to share the story and ask them to trust me, as their lead advisor. Because of the open, caring relationship we have always built with our clients, the transition was easier, built on trust and mutual respect, and with them knowing I had their best interest at heart.

The next few months were very difficult personally, but the clients saw none of it. We continued to take care of their needs and invest their money with their best interest in mind, while in the background, we dealt with the previous advisor going to prison, then attempting to take back the clients, once he was out. This was something he could not legally do, yet he pressured us. I experience some grief with this, as my trust was gone, and the freedom of my old life with it. Not only was I now a lead advisor, I had a partner and I was a small business owner. I was also still a mom and a wife, working to find balance between work and home and now having to put my children in daycare. I am so grateful I had such a supportive husband, who was at my side through all of this.

I never thought of myself as doing something to change the world, but as I look back on it today, I did make a difference in my clients' lives. I kept them whole, because changing advisors can be a very stressful thing, especially when you are forced to do so. It causes distrust for the profession and concern for the money that they worked so hard to save for retirement. An advisor helps create income for their retirement, helping them to cover their bills, both medical and mortgage. The income is vital to keeping the lights on and in some cases, helping future generations such as helping with a grandchild's college cost. If a client were forced to move their accounts, they would have to work with someone new, start the whole process over, find someone they trust and share their very personal and private information with them. It would cost them money in closing and transfer fees, and with a new advisor, they would have to learn about new investments and have to re-establish links to their bank for their income. It could be a very stressful disruption in their lives, especially for my older clients, and one they didn't deserve to experience, due to my boss's selfish and illegal acts. So that is why I kept their interests foremost in everything that I did, and I worked to protect them from the mistakes of their previous advisor.

The clients could have changed firms if they wanted, and a few did, but very few, instead most wanted to stay with "the girls" with whom they had worked, some for more than ten years. Now, ten years later, I have grown personally and professionally. I have purchased the firm from my partner, and I am honored and humbled each day that I now open the door to my own firm and look at the names of the people who I continue to call my clients and my friends, many of them still with me for over twenty years. I have continued to care for my clients, and their families, making home visits when they could no longer drive, visiting nursing homes and mourning losses and attending funerals, when they passed. I continue every day, knowing I have a job, a career and a purpose, because others believe in my skill, connect to my compassion, and trust me with their money and their legacy. For that, I will be forever grateful. That fateful day when I opened the door to the IRS, was the start of a crisis, but not one that would take me down, but instead, one that would challenge me to make a difference in my little part of the world.

Questions to Ponder

What would you do if you were suddenly forced into a position of leadership?

Would you tackle it, or would you defer to someone else?

What would you do not to waste a good crisis?

Author
Christine Rondeau, CFP
Financial Advisor
Investment Planners, Inc.
Neenah, Wisconsin

"Don't make money your goal. Instead, pursue the things you love doing."

Maya Angelou

Supporting Grace in Healthcare Moments

My name is Julie. I am a daughter, sister, wife, mother, cousin, friend, healthcare professional, community partner, and leader.

I am living and working in my city of origin and actually have an office in the hospital that I was born in. Not many people can say that!

For as long as I can remember, I have been "caregiving" seeking ways to bring comfort, support, healing to whoever was "in my path" or sphere of influence – whether it be family, friends, colleagues, community…I was there and wanted to make a difference wherever I could.

My role of child life specialist evolved as I matured and moved to new communities eventually settling back in my hometown. In my childhood I experienced surgery and healthcare experiences which contributed to my desire to help bridge transitions, preparation and support for children and families in varied healthcare settings. Looking at the whole family through varied perspectives and lenses—child, siblings, parents, extended family—helped me prepare for roles to advocate for pediatric pain management, individualized care plans, improvements in medical education and patient and family centered care.

Reducing anxiety and feelings of isolation through healing environments and community building opportunities is my passion. I have been privileged to be part of leading this work, creating opportunities and mentoring along the way, in a large academic medical community, I feel I have been able to make a difference through meeting each person right where they are, being present in the moment, ready to listen, respond and help guide action to improve and enhance the patient experience.

I truly believe in synergy, God-moments, and doing "small things with great love" as Mother Teresa would say. I feel I have been open to listen to God's calling and continually try to discern where He is leading me to help, to be.

I have watched and learned from others gleaning elements to fold into my own clinical practice and apply skills and lessons learned to both my personal and professional life.

I have utilized skills of observation and empathy to work together with a multidisciplinary team of healthcare professionals and patient-family advisors to create an individualized comfort plan to reduce pain and anxiety associated with needlesticks and procedures for children. Having a needlestick, while one of the most common healthcare experiences can be among the most traumatic for a child. This has been shown to carry over to adult experiences if the child is not taught coping strategies and skills to handle the procedure. Our work has now moved into the adult healthcare setting thanks to dedication from our team, and the repeated voice of pediatric patients who have transitioned to adult care settings and shared the need to have these resources from their childhood expanded for adults who may be afraid, pain and anxiety for similar procedures.

Again, it's often the "little things" like listening, asking preferences for watching or not watching, sitting up or laying down that can help an individual whether it's a child or an adult feel more comfortable and treated with dignity and respect. Hospitals may be common environments for the healthcare professionals who work in them. However, to a child or an adult who is a patient and their family, these are uncommon experiences and they need to have support from trained professionals to navigate these paths and increase their skills of self-advocacy.

This is what our program has provided and has been demonstrated to support. We have had other health systems ask for guidance to help them start a similar program. Our interdisciplinary team has discussed our efforts in national and international conference presentations. We also have taken these lessons learned and brought them to the public health setting at the community level through partnership with schools, museums and hospitals. This has proved to be a natural and beneficial setting: helping people especially children and families learn about and gain perspective about healthcare experiences through medical play and education in a comfortable setting in their own communities.

Questions to Ponder

How can you facilitate opportunities to find meaningful and compassionate outcomes in your place of influence whether it be in the community setting, your family or a place of employment?

What does grace in the moment mean to you?

How can you show honor by being truly present in your community, place of employment and/or your family?

Author
Julie R. Piazza, husband James,
3 sons: Christian, Graham and Landon
Senior Project Manager and Certified Child Life
Specialist, Michigan Medicine
Ann Arbor, Michigan

"Women can be powerful, graceful, and complex, with the ability to make any choice they desire."
Jessica Chastain

Working for the Almighty

My story actually starts with my husband, Rick. After being employed at the same company for 25 years he was feeling the need for a change. So, in March of 2017 he went to work for Diamond Vogel.

During their weekly maintenance meetings, it was brought up that the company was thinking about creating a cleaning position to give a little tender loving care to some of the areas that were starting to look a little neglected. It would be a position under the maintenance department. Rick, knowing that I have prior experience in the cleaning field, offered up me and my knowledge for the company.

Sometime in early October 2017, I met up with Dan, the guy responsible for creating this position and my husband's boss. Dan took me on a tour of the plant, showing me areas to be taken care of along with what he'd like to be done on a regular basis. We spent close to two hours discussing the details about what the job description could look like.

The end of December rolled around and I got a phone call from Dan. The position had been approved and there was now a formal job description written up that he would like me to stop by and look at. On the 28th, I went to look at what he had for the position's description and he asked me to change it as I saw fit, as he trusted my input. Everything looked as it should to me and I offered some advice on how they could try to find the right person for the job. He looked at me and asked, "You wouldn't want to do it, would you?" I responded, "Seriously?!" "Yeah," he said. I replied, "Let's call Rick in here to see what he thinks,"

Dan then radioed for Rick and a couple of minutes later, he walked in the door. I told him what Dan had come up with for the job and that he had offered it to me. Rick's response was, "Welcome aboard."

I left there that day with a job I didn't even know I wanted. I started working on January 8, 2018 and was excited for my first paycheck. The closer it got to pay day, the more I started wondering what I was going to do with all of this 'extra money.'

Previously, I had been a full-time farmer's wife for a part time farmer, and it was not exactly income producing, but I was okay with that. Being in the working world again, making money, and getting paid on a regular basis, I just couldn't come up with what I was going to be using this extra income for.

I mean, I sure thought of things, but nothing really grabbed me as this is what I needed to use this money for.

Pay day comes, Dan hands me my paycheck, and I knew instantly what I was going to use it for: "Kingdom Building Work." That is still what it is used for to this day. Whether it's paying for groceries, filling up a tank of gas, leaving generous tips, paying for car repairs, picking up the tab for the couple sitting next to us at the restaurant, or maybe picking up the tab for our entire table, helping pay for school supplies and lunch tickets, helping cover funeral expenses, or buying a room full of breast cancer survivors books at a retreat it's all been Spirit-led and I believe those acts of kindness are being used for "Kingdom Building".

You want to know the really cool part? When I accepted the job, I was scheduled to have pay raises every three months. When these times came, I received triple the amount that I was scheduled to get! Who does that? I'll tell you who. God.

Question to Ponder

How do you react when someone has been extremely generous to you?

Ponder this quote:

"Each one of us can make a difference. Together we make change."

Barbara Mikulski

Author
Andrea Theis
Husband: Rick
Children: Austin and Jessica
Work: Farmer and Corporate Cleaner for Diamond Vogel
Hopper, Iowa

Two Men and a Truck
from the Eyes of the Founder

In the early 80s I had three children, Melanie, Brig
and Jon. I was a newly single mom and my goal
that before they 'flew the nest', each would have a
college education, straight teeth and will have been
to Europe. I was a systems analyst for the state of
Michigan, working every day in downtown Lansing.
I was very shy. My nickname was "Pinky" because
I blushed all the time.

Brig and Jon did odd jobs with an old pickup truck
for spending money. We put a small ad in the Town
Courier and the first line in the ad was **Two Men
and a Truck**. I drew a cartoon logo for them—it is
still our logo. They charged $25 an hour. The boys
put a little of their money in an orange dish in the
kitchen for future ads and gas for the truck. It was
good spending money for them. Later, they went
away to college with my blessing, I hired two men,

bought an old cube van for $350 and 'officially' started **Two Men and a Truck.** That $350 was all my savings and the only money I ever invested in the company.

The truck was so old - it constantly broke down. I had never supervised anyone and wasn't very good at it - (call it the tail wagging the dog). I recorded incoming calls on an answering machine and would come home on my lunch hour, checking to see if there were any calls. One day there were 12 calls! We moved people all over in that old truck, Detroit, Traverse City, Ohio.

The next year I bought a new little truck, but it wasn't easy. The salesman wanted to know if my husband would sign for me. No husband. Yikes! I persevered and then started adding a new truck every year. The more trucks we had on the road, the more 'moving billboards' we had and the more customers we attracted.

One day, the state police pulled our truck over because we didn't have a moving license. I didn't know anything about a license, so I drew a circle on the map with a soup can and told the movers not to go outside of the circle. Then a state policewoman came to my home and wanted to see my paperwork. I remember she had blue eye shadow, so I felt she would do me no harm. Wrong! She found seven moves that were outside of our legal area and wrote me seven misdemeanor tickets in my living room! I had to hire an attorney, go to court and my picture was in the paper. My attorney asked why I let her in to look at my paperwork - she didn't have a warrant. How would I know? She seemed very nice.

We parked the trucks in my Mom's back yard. She kept her eye on them through her windows and would let me know if the men were late for work and things like that. The men liked her, though. One day she slipped on the ice trying to fill her bird feeders. The movers found her and helped her in the house - broken glasses and a bent nose. They were so worried. Everyone called her Grandma Eb. We had business cards made for her, "Helen Eberly, Yard Boss". She was in her late 80s but helped me in every way she could.

People started telling me I should 'franchise' my little moving business. I didn't understand franchising. There weren't any books about it back then. One friend had me talk to a local franchising attorney and he got me started. First, we had to protect the name **Two Men and a Truck**. It was very difficult, as the big movers used that phrase as a tag line, but after years, we finally succeeded in protecting the name nationwide. I franchised the company in 1988.

In 1989, Jon graduated from college. I had met my personal parenting goals. I took the giant leap. I quit my day job. It was a hard decision. I had worked for the state for 20 years, was making good money back then 'for a woman' and enjoyed five weeks of paid vacation annually. Everyone was either worried about me or making fun of me.

Melanie was living in Atlanta. I convinced her in to start her own **Two Men and a Truck** and she became my first franchisee. Later, Brig and Jon opened their own franchises in Ishpeming and Grand Rapids. Melanie, Jon and I started to do franchise shows. We did four the first year. We didn't have much of a booth - a card table, tablecloth and a TV I borrowed that would play a 60 second ad repeatedly.

Two Men and a Truck continued to grow. I hired employees and added more franchisees. I moved the office from my dining room table into an old gas station on Kalamazoo Street in Lansing in 1990. In 1991 I rented a two-room office in an old house on Michigan Avenue for our franchising office.

That winter I slipped on the ice and broke my leg. It was a Saturday and after I left the emergency room, I went home and worked on my books, laying on the couch with my cast up in the air. By Monday, I was back at the office. When you own a business, there are no 'sick days' (unlike working for the state!).

We were always broke. I never had any book-keeping classes. I kept a shoe box under my desk labeled "INS AND OUTS." My bills. When I had money, I would pay them.

In 1994 the Republican party asked me to run for the state Senate. I had never been in politics before and was very excited. I asked Melanie, now living in Michigan, to take over the franchising office. We had 36 franchises then. I asked Jon to come and run the Lansing **Two Men and a Truck** which had several trucks and employees. They both had their own lives, families, moving companies and had to drive 60 miles to come to Lansing, almost daily, and I didn't have any money to pay them! My political career didn't last too long. I didn't care for it. The party found someone else to run for office in my place. I returned to TMT, but Melanie remained as President.

My older son, Brig, was living in the UP [Upper Peninsula, Michigan] with his wife, Francine and three children. We asked him to come and help us. In 1996 they sold everything, Fran left her teaching job and they moved back down state. We could barely pay Brig.

We slowly took over the whole old house for our franchise offices and in 1998 built a new building in Okemos. In six months, we had outgrown our new building. In 2002 we built a larger office, outgrew it and added on in 2004. The building has been greatly enlarged since then.

We signed up for the Adopt-A-Highway program and sponsored a baseball team. In 2000 we started donating 10¢ from each move to the American Cancer Society - this resulted in hundreds of thousands of dollars for charities. We still do it today.

Melanie ran the company for 12 years and in 2008, she stepped aside to spend time with her family. Brig took over as CEO and is still in that position today. Jon is very active on many state and national boards. He also worked with lobbyists to upgrade the state moving laws. We now have thousands of trucks and employees in the United States, Canada and Europe.

In 2017 I retired. It was an exciting journey for me and my family and we feel extremely blessed. These are the lessons I learned:

Lesson 1 - Even if you are shy, you can do public speaking if you do it enough.

Lesson 2 - Always give back to your community.

Lesson 3 - The Customer ALWAYS comes first!

Lesson 4 - Love what you do - life is not a dress rehearsal.

Lesson 5 - Don't listen to negative comments.

Lesson 6 - Even if you are broke, let people know you WILL pay them back. Keep in contact with them. Give others as much as you can afford every month.

Lesson 7 - Always say YES! to any opportunity, because you don't know where it will lead you.

Lesson 8 - Don't lose your focus.

Lesson 9 - Take lots of pictures! You will be so glad some day you did. It's easy now with an iPhone.

Lesson 10 - If you want to do something bad enough, you can make it happen. Even if you can only do a little each day, do something! When you look back, you will see you have accomplished a lot!

Questions to Ponder

Do you think it would be easier to do this today?

Would you be open to someone challenging you to do something you thought could make a difference?

Ponder this quote.

"Goodness is about character - integrity, honesty, kindness, generosity, moral courage, and the like. More than anything else, it is about how we treat other people."

Dennis Prager

Author
Mary Ellen Sheets
Founder of Two Men and a Truck
Retired in Venice, Florida
Originally from Okemos, Michigan

Tuesday Surprises!

Not long ago, on a cold Tuesday Morning, I looked across the field toward the abandoned Festival sheds and saw the small form of a shivering human being, huddling in the early morning sun. It was Jorge, a 68-year-old Farmworker.

The day before, Jorge had fainted in the fields 60 miles from our center and was taken to the local Hospital. After assessment and re-hydration, he was placed in a courier car and sent to our Center with a note pinned to his hospital Gown, "Take to Sister Nancy, she'll know what to do with him."

The courier had dropped him off in the empty parking lot late Monday afternoon after we closed and left him there. He spent the cold night in the shed with just his trousers and hospital gown for a cover. He had a temperature of 103, was congested, and was short of breath.

So, I began my day at our Centro de los Pobres, the Center for the Poor. Tuesdays, which always hold surprises, it's the only day we are closed. It allows all volunteers to make appointments and catch up on the needs of their own farmworker families. I make the trip from Pueblo to check the mail and bring deliveries collected at my home. It also gives me time to think and do some necessary book work without the necessary interruptions associated with our work.

Jorge was, as many are today, an elderly farmworker with no home in which to live. The workers pour into our county for fieldwork hoping to find a place to stay. But first, they must make enough money to pay for it. Jorge had moved from shed to shed, relying on his wits to find food, water and shelter and work. A trip to the ER, IV's, antibiotics and a warm bed helped him to recover.

On another Tuesday morning, not much later, I arrived at the Center, to find a car of four young workers waiting in the parking lot. Lying in the back seat was Joel, a 21-year-old worker who had fallen from a roof in Tennessee. They had taken him to the nearest ER but were turned away because he had no insurance. The employer had denied them compensation.

On the urging of a relative in our area, the young men had driven 36 hours to bring their injured friend to our center. Joel was in agony; the trip had been excruciating. I sent him right into the emergency room. His back was badly fractured, and he required an instrumented fusion. Upon recovery he returned to roofing despite the inherent dangers and continued to send money home to his parents. He would never consider himself being labeled "disabled."

I am Nancy Crafton, a Sister of Charity of Cincinnati. Formally a Clinical Nurse Specialist and now a "Madrecita" or little Mother to our families. I operate a small non-profit in Avondale, Colorado, a community of farms and farmworkers.

I began this work in 1994 while working at our hospital. Our chaplain, Maurice Gallagher, was also the pastor of the small church in the farming community. He tried to help the families as best he could.

Visiting him one evening in 1994 I witnessed the steady traffic of workers into his pantry for food and clothing. He knew immediately that he needed organization. I decided to help.

We set up a small room and built shelves and racks for food and hang clothes. I sought grants from my community for food and asked for volunteers to take care of the room for two days a week and four hours.

In 2000, I decided it was time to move into this secondary ministry full-time. I applied for non-profit status and moved the operation from the rectory to a "shed" built behind the church. I had one light bulb and a garage door. When the darkness came, I would move my truck into the doorway and turn on the lights so we could see!!

On opening day, we assisted 120 families, many of whom we had never served before. They were coming from all over for help, for food, clothing, medical and legal care. They also wanted help registering their children for school. Eventually we outgrew our small shed and with the help of a grant, built a large warehouse structure which became our new place of service.

We have registered over 16,000 families in the 19 years of our existence. We are an all-volunteer service, continuing to provide food, clothing, household goods, medical and legal care and, of course, education. We now have several college graduates.

Because our clients are, for the most part undocumented, they are not allowed to have health insurance. Connecting them to care has become a major part of our service at this time in our history, cancers, fractures, surgeries, diabetes, kidney failure and high blood pressure, all contribute to major costs. Los Pobres networks with hospitals and providers for help.

There are many misconceptions about undocumented workers in our country today. Americans seem to no longer have their historical memories. America's early involvement in wars brought many workers from Mexico and Central America into our country, initially to manage the farm work. When the wars ended, the workers were deported, so that the returning soldiers could have their jobs. The deportations included American children, born to those men and women who lived and worked in our fields.

Today those "children" are 60, 70, and 80 years old. Proving their citizenship has been a challenge with poorly kept or non-existing documents.

In 2000 President George Bush and Mexico's then President, Vicente Fox, began a wonderful program of bringing the workers out of the shadows and into American society. Applications for residency were in full-swing and benefitted a great number of our families and children. They were beginning to come out of the shadows and into full membership within our society, and then 9/11 happened.

After 9/11, they became the enemies, the terrorist, the unwanted, and again, the invisible workers. Drivers licenses from their own countries were confiscated and could no longer be used for identifications or for driving. Birth certificates for newborns could not be obtained without legal documents. Bank accounts could not be opened without official, state sanctioned identification. All these requirements meant existing here with "papers" Papers our families did not have. Driving children to and from school, to work, to appointments meant being arrested if stopped. This meant fines and possible deportation if ICE was notified.

Today, in 2019, we are faced with different Hardships. DACA recipients (Deferred Action for Childhood Arrivals) have become pawns for the current administration. Deportation of clients who have lived here since infancy, is a real and current danger. Suggesting that our clients should now be feared because they are from Mexico; Central and South America is unconscionable. We at Los Pobres continue to demonstrate the goodness of our hardworking families and the economic profits that they bring to our country.

Questions to Ponder

What are we as professional members of the Catholic Church doing to help our invisible and forgotten brothers and sister?

Where does our church stand on immigration issues?

What help is the church providing in substance?

Author
Sister Nancy R. Crafton, S.C.
Sister of Charity of Cincinnati, Ohio
Live and works in Colorado

"Happiness is having a large, loving, caring, close-knit family in another city."
George Burns

Heart Sent Butterflies

Ever since I was a young child, I have seen hearts. A random rock on a trail, the rain that had collected from the down spout that spilled onto the hot pavement, the potato chip, all in a shape of a heart. Once there was a discarded plastic bag that made its final destination after soaring through the air in a bush. The handles caught on the thorny branches, closed together, the bag filled with the breeze, and became the shape of a heart. Those hearts have always given me the message of pure, unconditional love.

I am riding in the back seat of my mother's Malibu. A brown eyed, brown haired ballerina, a boney little first grader. Soft maroon seats, I place my hands on the sun that is flowing in on the seat next to me. I trace the heart shape that the sun's rays are somehow making for me. I have never been alone. My Guardian Angel, Arch Angels, loved ones on the other side, Mother Mary, so many visited me and always have. I am blessed with the knowledge of this pure love that is given so freely. I knew then as a young child how special it was. I knew innately that I was special. I look out the window wondering what my purpose was to be. Even at six years old I knew I was meant to share this pure love on a great level. Mesmerized by whatever captivates my glance in those quick seconds while the car sped down the road. I still do this, look out the window and see all that I can see. Everything is an educational moment for me. Images become knowledge; words read on signs pose questions of wonderment. I was a dreamer. Full of love for life because that is all I knew. Some have said that I do not miss a thing, I take in all the details like a great life detective. I would find out what all the hearts meant. I was a determined young lady.

The innocence of life came to an abrupt stop a year later when my maternal grandmother was diagnosed with throat cancer. I had already been tagging along with my mother who was a caregiver for an aging couple, so I was prepared to swing into action just as my mother was. She and I would drive down to Toledo every weekend when I got home from school and stay with Grandma. My Mother and I watched her die. That woman was graceful even in her last breaths. The cancer ate away at her throat, so she wrapped a silk scarf around it. It was a lot for a young girl of six to see. I wouldn't change a thing. The image of my mother holding my grandmother up in the shower burned into my memory. The love we gave my grandmother was so easy. One spring afternoon in 1984 my grandmother asked me to lie in bed with her. At this point she could no longer form words. The cancer was oozing black matter out of her neck. She wanted me to just lie with her as I am sure she contemplated death. I did, but not without fear of being near the thing that was taking her away from me. I look back now and think how brave I was. Somehow, I knew that it was what she needed. Unconditional love from a little girl on her death bed.

A few months later I watched tragically as my brother drowned on a day that was supposed to be a celebration. It had only a fraction of a second that we were all at the funeral home and now we were back. A blink of an eye that he was there and then not. My brother was only 15 years old, one-month shy of his 16th birthday. I had never known so much anguish before then. Anguish because of the amount of love that we felt we lost. Love that we felt we were unable to give any longer to our loved ones. Love that we felt we would never get back or be replaced. I understand now that that was all an illusion. We never loose love. They never stop loving us as we most certainly never stop loving them. We just put the hugging and kissing on hold till we reunite in Heaven.

What I did learn over the years with continuous deaths in each year of my life was that love did always come back. I have had so many deaths, more than any births, because I continue to love so many people. Everything that I have done in my life has been about love. Those hearts. As I pondered my purpose during those formable years, I began to realize that any career I picked I would be successful. ANY CAREER. I could have taken all the grief in my life, all the loss and let it destroy my faith. Death could have killed my determination to serve in the name of love. I threw myself more into my passions of dance and music. After all, healing comes in many shapes. St. Joan of Arc wouldn't have let me give up anyway.

When my childhood best friend died, I happened to be pregnant with my first-born. I took that time in my life to be the best mother that I could be. The deaths of my two most impactful schoolteachers gave me the drive to be the best educator.

In my twenties I knew that I was destined to be a teacher. I learned over the years that it came in many avenues. I didn't have to only be a teacher in the grade school traditional way to be considered a "teacher." I taught ballet and gave my passion for the arts to the students. I taught at an "at risk" middle school youth how to make sense out of life during tough years. Love came in the shape of a heart, in the shape of a pencil, a computer, ballet slippers, and in support of someone else's dreams.

As the years went on I began to realize that I needed to touch more hearts with this infinite love.

My Guardian Angel continued to nudge me in the correct direction as I contemplated my greater purpose. I knew I was a teacher, but I sensed there was more.

As I approached my forties, I began to redefine myself. I had been teaching at the local YMCA for about ten years, water aerobics and other various classes. Countless men and women there have touched my soul, inspired me, and supported me. They still to this day tell me how I have done the same for them! Simple synchronicity lined me up with my desire to focus on that feeling I had when I was a young girl. I was special, and it was time for my identity commitment. I allowed myself to believe that I was more than a teacher and realized I was a healer as well. Love heals!

In addition to the exercise program that I created that helped reshape the way my students formerly thought about themselves, I began to study reflexology and reiki. The birth of my business began. I would teach, guide and lead people how to find their healing paths through love and support. Attaining goals together, with unconditional motivating love. I gained all my necessary schoolings from accredited institutions and dreamed up my business name. Chrysalis Reflexology and Fitness Consulting.

You see, not only do I have hearts come to me as divine messages, I also have butterflies. Butterflies were so fitting. We go through this path in life where we struggle. Often, we fear we may be eaten by the predator. We manage to make it to where we can form this chrysalis around us and withdraw in contemplation of our journey. At the right time, not under our control, but with the right amount of patience and determination we emerge. Beautiful as a butterfly! Only we can dream up our colors, the size of our wingspan, how high we can fly, where we go!

I choose to use the butterfly as my business logo because our heart should always be present, in EVERYTHING that we do. The butterfly reminds us that our journey is unique to us. Some of us make it, some of us sadly do not realize that we have unconditional love at our fingertips.

I can say with full confidence that I make a difference every day in my work. Not just because my clients constantly verbalize this, but because I see it in their actions. It is like a chain of productivity. We make a difference in each other's lives because we continuously provide a no judgment, safety zone full of hearts and butterflies. We remain childlike together, all of us inter-generational friends finding healing within each other. They keep me going as much as I keep them going because we can trust each other's love in its pureness.

We all have lost much in life. However, in death we eventually find rebirth. I am born to lead with love and help guide others to find their healing journey inside and out.

Questions to Ponder

Ask your true self, what barrier has kept me separated from giving and receiving love?

What is keeping me from the full achievement of success that I do rightly or fully deserve?

You are the caterpillar inside the chrysalis. Let the caterpillar feel the love and become the beautiful butterfly it was intended to be.

Author
Laurie Ann DeBruin, CRR, CCH, BA
Owner and Founder Chrysalis Reflexology & Fitness Consulting LLC, Certified and Registered Reflexology Practitioner, Certified Group Fitness Instructor, Cancer Exercise Specialist, Certified Consulting Hypnotist, Usui Holy Fire Reiki Master, Vaganova Classical Ballerina, Inspirational Speaker/Author/Psychic Medium
Okemos, Michigan

"The butterfly
counts not months
but moments and
has time enough."

Rabindranath Tagore

82

Living is Your Giving

I am a lover of life! My passion is people and I can't meet enough of them! I'm addicted to those spontaneous conversations where strangers become friends! Because of this, I've always known I needed a job where I am surrounded by people, to satisfy that hunger! For this reason, my quest began, first in thought, and then in fruition. That's the way anything is birthed. Everything that ever was, first was a thought. (So, think good thoughts!)

I was at a point in my life where I needed change. I wanted to 'make a difference' instead of only making money. The satisfaction I received from the previous business I owned was fading. Quite honestly, I was restless, bored, unsatisfied, thinking, "Is this it?" What I soon realized was I had limiting beliefs! Digging into books, Ted talks and motivational sermons and talking with friends and acquaintances taught me what I now know as I write, the song sung by Rod Stewart comes to mind: "I wish that I knew what I know now when I was younger." Time is precious and keeps on ticking, so use it well!

Reading has been a huge influencer in the direction I've taken. Strengths Finder 2.0, which is a popular personality test, has been very instrumental in that it teaches one to focus on his/her strengths, rather than weaknesses. Sounds like teachings from preschool but how many of us focus on the one thing wrong, instead of the forty things right? I harnessed this information and brought it into my family as well as a gathering that meets at our house. I asked everyone to give me their contact information and beside their name share their gifts or talents. Something that I thought was a simple request ended in many blank spaces after their names. People didn't know what their gifts were.

After some study, I have come to believe that God leaves clues! I also believe that if you don't know what your gifts are, you don't know what your purpose is. Your gifts and talents are what God gave you at birth, and that is 'what comes naturally easy for you.' Most don't think of their gift as anything special because they think, 'everybody can do this' and I'm here to tell you that's far from the truth. This gift was given to you, 'specifically' and you need to bring it to the world! People are waiting for you to share this gift, because they need to experience it! You may be the one thing that opens the door to their believing they can do it!

I'm reminded of the stories that came out in the newspapers a year after 9/11 happened. The people who had been affected by 9/11 lost their spouses, their jobs, their purpose, their everything. Interestingly enough, a year later some of these survivors were reborn through the horrific events. The pain crushed some while others were catapulted into lives of total gratification. How? They went back to all they knew, what they possessed, their gifts and talents!! Some went back to their first love, a job they had in the past, only now, they were the boss. Others found themselves in their dream jobs doing what they love, that thing that made their hearts sing and were truly satisfied.

This made me delve inside myself to find what I could do with what I'd been given. I knew I had two constants in my life, the love of people and creativity, now all I had to do was combine them and create a job...my mind went blank for quite some time. I had thoughts that spiraled me downward and then remembered that 'thoughts become things' and switched my thinking to more positive paths. I also remember telling the group that met at our house I would be using my gifts in my barn and asked them to hold me accountable. That was exactly the pressure I needed.

I wasn't quite sure what or when, but I did know I wanted to lead by example. I went out to my big red barn and began the long and stinky cleanup. I decided to make a room in the barn a creative space, so I could have a garage sale to get rid of all of the items left from the last owners. I had six weekends of garage sales and in that time, magic happened! Remember my cravings for spontaneous conversation? Well, I found it with all these people coming to my barn. During the time of the sales, people asked, "Can I consign some art work here?" and "Why is this so cute if you're not a store, it's such a good location?" I told a few people, "I'm just a barn sale," but then, I started thinking, and started taking contact information and people's medium or talent. I talked with my husband and the following summer, I tried it on, committing to Saturdays only. I still ran it like a barn sale but did it throughout the entire summer and it was well received.

I was off to a discombobulated start!! I had no idea what I was doing but claimed "ignorance on fire," and still do at times, but I'm failing forward as I take steps towards more ideas to bring into fruition!! The second year we changed our hours, I was open five days a week and renovated another room. We had a guy from Uganda move in with us and later I found that he played twelve instruments!! The third year I changed the new room into what I called "The Jazz Room" because our house guest liked jazz and played it oh so well.

My husband had been doing mission work and came home showing me pictures of garbage dump cities in the Philippines, where people got dumped when they didn't have anywhere to live. I remember this sticking in my head and God working in my heart as well. Thoughts of these people being thrown in the garbage, along with the trash, haunted me until one day a revelation was given. I felt that inner prompting saying, "If this bothers you so much, what are you going to do about it?" I looked around my store and many of the artists' work was made from stuff and junk, dismantled, altered and redesigned - upcycled, repurposed or reclaimed works of art. Lightbulb moment!! I decided that if the people lived in the garbage, why not redesign the garbage into sellable items to gain them sustainability? It was like "when life hands you lemons, make lemonade" idea.

I told my husband I wanted to go with him on the next trip. I flew for thirty-six hours, took five planes and one bumpy Jeepney to find my heart's desire! The people of the garbage dump city were in sight and I was ready to empower them to believe that they didn't have to settle for the lifestyle they were living. There was more, so much more, for them.

Ironically, as I was on my way to the garbage dump from the house I was staying in, I spotted a seller's market. I jumped out, gathered information and found that anybody can sell whatever they want and there was no fee. I had to smile...it was a total God thing. Only God can set something up so perfectly! I proceeded to the dump and set up to teach. People began slowly coming into the bamboo building, all of them with their heads down, making no eye contact, feeling like the trash they lived amongst. I was in my element, because there were humans before me and so I started showing them, via a translator, how to make things out of their trash. Not until I showed them how to crochet plastic bags into bedrolls did they see the light! My translator stopped translating and all I heard was their Cebuano tongue, crying and laughing!! My husband was filming me and I looked at him and his look said, "This is crazy!" and I thought, "No, that's hope!" They got it. They realized they could make sellable items as well as items to make their lives easier. The possibilities!

I wake up every day and think of my Filipino friends and how I can help make a positive difference in their lives. The Filipino garbage dump dwellers are one of the reasons for my store. Nobody is a throw away in my book! I found that they can make trash into sellable items, make money to have a sustainable life, feel good about that fact and become a piece of art themselves!! Transformed people from transformed trash!!! They are beautiful, talented people and it's my mission to help them believe it.

I have been in business for six years with the seventh coming up and we have grown from a one room barn sale to: selling art, music and enter-tainment, art classes, mission work, weddings, room rental, an outdoor event space, Ted-talks-like barn talks. Farm to Table dining is currently in the works. Transformations Art Barn is a business where "We're more than a store, we transform lives through Art and Entertainment!" Our hope is to help you transform your life and then transform the world with your God given gifts! Remember the world is waiting! Don't die with your song still needing to be sung! Sing out Loud!

There's more in store for us and you. To the future growth of you and everyone! Charge!

My hope is that you'll 'Live in your gifting' and share them with the world!

Questions to Ponder

What will you do with the gifts you possess?

Will you let your gifts lay, anxiously awaiting use, or will you realize their potential and give them life?

Author
Sandy Dow Haga
Transformations Art Barn
South Haven, Michigan

A Powerful Gift
Praying Together

God uses the ordinary so that He can do the extraordinary. I am one of the 'ordinary' that wants to grow in my faith, and understand God's calling in my life. My friends are also 'ordinary' but when we gather together in His name, the extraordinary happens. When we give God our 'yes,' God does the rest.

I was born and raised in a Catholic family in Michigan. Upon receiving my college degree, I began working in international business. I married in 1994 and moved to the Chicago area, becoming a stay-at-home mom to four beautiful children. Unfortunately, in 2009, my marriage dissolved, and my life took a turn. As I turned to God for support and comfort, God slowly began revealing His desires for me.

Growing up, my family always had a strong devotion to the Blessed Mother. In 2010, after my separation, I went on a pilgrimage to Medjugorje, an apparition site of the Virgin Mary, to pray for emotional healing. I remember so clearly, reading a message from Our Lady from September 25, 2000 that said:

"Dear children! Today I call you to open yourselves to prayer. May prayer become joy for you. Renew prayer in your families and form prayer groups. In this way, you will experience joy in prayer and togetherness. All those who pray and are members of prayer groups are open to God's will in their hearts and joyfully witness God's love. I am with you, I carry all of you in my heart and I bless you with my motherly blessing. Thank you for having responded to my call."

It struck me in a unique way and those words lingered and remained close to my heart, "form prayer groups." I couldn't shake them, and pondered the Blessed Mother's words for a year before finally taking action.

It began with getting together with girlfriends to pray the rosary. As time went by, it evolved into a deeper encounter with God. Now, we meet every Monday to begin the week with prayer (and some socializing and eating too!). The structure of our prayer time is this: We begin by praising and thanking God for the opportunity to spend time with Him. We pray with and for each other and our families, followed by prayers for all those who have asked us to pray for them. We then do a *lectio divina* (a meditation) on the upcoming Sunday's gospel, coming up with tangible ways to apply the living word in our lives. Whether it's praying the prayer of humility each morning that week, or conscientiously bringing the love of Jesus (with a loving smile or word) to every cashier, grocery store attendant or postal worker, or spending time infront of Jesus in adoration, our goal is action focused.

We have seen so many fruits as a result of praying together as a group. First, the power of storming heaven with our intentions, our prayers united, has brought comfort, consolation and healing to us, and so many whom we pray for. Our prayers are never left unanswered, we are confident of that.
In praying together, we support one another.
In moments of celebration, we praise God together and give thanks, and when someone is going through a difficult circumstance and cannot pray, we pray for them.

There is an indescribable comfort that comes with praying together each and every week. Our crosses that we carry seem lighter, and our joyous moments seem more glorious.

As the years pass, we continue to pray and discern what the Holy Spirit is asking of us, individually and as a group. We know God brought us together for a purpose, and as time goes by, we see Gods' plan unfold. God has placed beautiful priests in our path, some as spiritual directors while sending others with beautiful gifts of healing. In spiritual direction, we continue to learn about the truths of our faith, including the incredible love of Jesus and His mercy that is immeasurable. We share our faith journey together, learn from each other's experiences and pray with and for each other.

After personally receiving a physical healing by Jesus through the prayers of Fr. Ubald, our group was inspired. When witnessing the healing power of God, you want to share it with the world. We were moved by the Holy Spirit to action.

One of our missions is inviting Father each year, coordinating countless masses with healing prayers in the Chicago land area. On an evening when the church would otherwise be empty, anywhere from 500-1,000 people gather (Catholic and not) to pray for healing.

These beautiful nights of healing would not be possible without the encouragement and help of every person in the prayer group. We have seen people healed of cancer, healed of HIV, we've seen the deaf hear, the lame rise up from their wheel-chairs. Tumors have disappeared, broken marriages restored, the grace of forgiveness given, addictions shattered.

Our awesome God wants to heal us, and the signs and wonders are all around. I'll never forget the 10 year old girl who was born with spina bifida. She walked in with her grandmother, mother, sister and aunt. She came in leaning on her grandma with braces on her feet as one was completely turned in, she had severe bladder control issues, was born deaf among other major health problems. During adoration after the mass, she signed to her mom that she had to use the bathroom. She was able to go to the bathroom on her own, and as she walked out, her legs completely straightened. She looked at her mom and for the first time, could hear her voice. She ran up and down the aisles and couldn't remove the smile from her face, as her sister cried with joy.

We believe the Holy Spirit, along with our sweet Mother Mary, has inspired our prayer group to evangelize and be witnesses of God's love.

Whether it's organizing a morning of reflection for the parish, or handing out countless books about our faith, or running Eucharistic adoration at the church,or organizing masses with healing prayers, we all support each other, encourage each other, lift each other up and grow in our faith together. As Jesus sent His disciples two by two, we also feel the power and impact of praying and working together, to increase our faith and trust in God, and to bring it to others. We see and feel what Our Lady said in her message, we do experience joy in prayer and togetherness, we do witness God's love when we gather, and as a result, we are open to God's will in our hearts. Thank you, Jesus for the fruits of sisterhood and praying together.

Questions to Ponder

When in your life have you felt a nudge from the Holy Spirit, or had a lingering thought that you just couldn't shake. Did you act on it? What fruits have come from it?

Have you ever witnessed the healing power of Jesus, big or small? Why is it helpful to share those miracle stories with others?

How have you witnessed God's love in others?

Author
Monique Stevens
Stay-at-Home Mom
Glenview, Illinois

"When we give God our 'yes,' God does the rest."

Monique Stevens

Second Chances

On Tuesday morning, January 8, 2019, I was sitting on my patio, enjoying the Florida sun, watching my friend and work partner, Desmond Meade, register to vote on Facebook Live. Over two decades had passed since he had lost his voting rights due to previous drug-related felony convictions. On this day, he was one of 1.4 million people in Florida who had just gotten their voting rights restored. I was witnessing his vision manifested, his dream made reality.

I called to congratulate him. He answered excitedly, in his booming voice, "Do you see what we did Mila?! Do you see what we started?!" I laughed out loud, and responded, *"Yes! It feels like we just made amends with society for all of the crap we did when we were using."* And it was true. Although we were different ages, races and genders, Desmond and I had each been afflicted with the same disease of addiction, an illness that had once rendered us useless to our families, friends, employers and community members. But by the grace of God, we had been given a second chance in life through recovery, and in so doing, were able to spend seven years in partnership to make certain our friends across the state were given a second chance, as well.

Together, we catalyzed independent political power in Florida, building a grassroots movement that successfully amended the state's constitution, lifting the 150-year lifetime ban on, and restoring voting rights to, 1.4 million Floridians with past felony convictions through a multi-year, non-partisan, citizen-led, ballot initiative. This was a feat that no one believed was possible. This is my story of how it came to be.

I was born in 1981 into an immigrant family - my mother, Mexican and Catholic, my father, Lebanese and Muslim. My mother grew up a caretaker in an alcoholic home and my father grew up a witness to domestic abuse and religious rigidity. These are the traumas that they experienced, brought with them into the marriage and inevitably passed on to their children, as is often the case when generational pain goes unhealed.

My parents divorced when I was three. Both remarried and had two more children by the time I was 11. I was now the oldest of five, with two sets of parents, with conflicting worldviews, cultural norms and socio-economic status. I lived with my stepfather, who was a problem drinker and my mother, who suffered from untreated depression. Life was not easy, but I excelled in school, sports and work, always an overachiever, determined to one day escape my family situation. I did not realize that I was already sick, having been exposed to the family disease of alcoholism and mental illness. The only way I was ever going to be truly free was by going through an internal transformation that would only unfold after hitting rock bottom - something that would not come to me for another 15 years.

I attended university and earned a BS in Political Science. By my senior year, I was a full-blown addict to prescription painkillers. What started out as a great solution for chronic neck pain, turned into a four-year nightmare. At 22, I graduated, cum laude, then checked myself into detox. Although I knew I had a problem with opiates, I did not believe that alcohol was a drug, nor did I accept help from the recovery community. I was determined to handle this problem on my own and wanted no part of a spiritual solution.

From 2004 to 2011, I worked for the Michigan Democratic Party, fully indoctrinated in establishment politics and campaign organizing. I learned invaluable skills around data, field, fundraising and communications, but eventually became disenchanted and left Michigan to move to

Florida, hoping to start a new career that had nothing to do with politics or campaigns.
That was not what the universe intended for me because three months into my new job as Fund Development and Operations Coordinator with PICO National Network (PICO), I found myself at the center of my first ballot initiative campaign and had just met Desmond Meade. He was sharing his story and talking about felon disenfranchisement.

Here is what I learned: In Florida, if you had a felony conviction, you lost your eligibility to vote for life, even after completing your full sentence. Florida was one of only four states that did this, and at the time, 1.69 million people in the state were denied voting rights, as a result. That was 10% of Florida's voting population, with a disparate impact of 23% on Florida's Black voting population. This law was enshrined in Florida's Constitution, in 1838, in the immediate aftermath of the Civil War, when former confederate states had to amend their constitution to extend the right to vote to newly freed slaves to be reinstated to the Union. In response, Florida (and other southern states) created laws barring people with felony convictions from voting, while also expanding felony crimes in the penal code, to sustain slave labor through mass incarceration.

This blew my mind. I had found my calling and I was all in, fully committed to dismantling institutionalized racism in Florida and shifting the power dynamics in the state, forever.

After gaining critical experience in ballot initiative work in 2012, I spent 2013 trying to figure out how to blend electoral and community organizing methods more effectively. I discovered that by elevating support staff at the grassroots level, we could increase productivity and capacity statewide. As a result, we developed more effective communications and mobilization systems, integrated data-driven voter engagement tools, built a more diverse fund development portfolio and centralized operational functions to avoid duplication of work. This became the blueprint for success when we were finally able to launch the Second Chances ballot initiative campaign in 2018.

In 2014, Desmond and I were teamed up to advance the work for voting restoration and underwent a 12-month process to: 1) develop strategies and a campaign plan that would produce a win, but would also lift-up directly impacted people and create lasting grassroots infrastructure in the state; 2) craft sound policy in collaboration with diverse stakeholders (50+ organizations) that would pass judicial scrutiny, produce intended impact and protect implementation; and 3) drive participatory research for values-based messaging, to establish a viable path to victory. We achieved all three objectives that year.

Momentum was building, but my neck condition had worsened and after 10 years being off prescription drugs, I started using narcotics again for pain management, arrogantly believing I could control my use.

Immediately, I began abusing them, activating a compulsive cycle of binging, detoxing and withdrawing every four weeks for two years straight. No one knew what was going on with me, but my mood swings increased in intensity, and in September 2014, I was let go from PICO for being "toxic to the environment."

I was devastated and so was Desmond. We had finally proved that we could win, now everything came crashing down. For all of 2015, Desmond was the lone man standing. Partners left, funding dried-up and the organization imploded. His only support was from the grassroots volunteers who continued to collect petitions for two years to reach the 78K signatures required to trigger the legal review by the Florida Supreme Court to determine if the ballot language was deemed constitutional. During that time, Desmond single-handedly drove across the state dropping off blank petitions, picking up signed petitions and delivering them to the 68 county supervisors of elections offices across the state.

In July 2015, I quit taking painkillers and in September created The Wheelhouse Project, LLC. In early 2016, Desmond secured funding to hire me as a consultant to set-up the infrastructure and governing systems for the ballot initiative committees. I pulled this off, but my drinking was escalating without the drugs, and I was becoming a liability to Desmond rather than an asset. By August 2016, I knew I needed professional help, I could no longer be a slave to my addictions. I told Desmond I was checking myself into a rehab facility and he said, "about time." Desmond had already been in recovery for decades and had been patiently waiting for me to hit my bottom. I finally received my "gift of desperation" and was ready to gut out the pain I had been stuffing for years and become a willing and active participant in my own healing and spiritual awakening.

I completed detox, residential treatment, intensive outpatient treatment and worked the 12 steps of recovery with my sponsor. Meanwhile, Desmond submitted the 100,000 signatures collected by volunteers to trigger the Florida Supreme Court review and continued checking in with me to see if or when I was ready to come back.

In April 2017, at eight months clean and sober, Desmond informed me that the Florida Supreme Court unanimously approved the ballot language, that new polling had confirmed a 10% increase in public opinion about the amendment, and that he'd just secured funding to build out the Florida Rights Restoration Coalition (FRRC) - the state's only organization led for, and by, directly impacted people. Now, we needed to collect an additional one million petition signatures to qualify for the 2018 ballot. He said, *"I went out and got you everything you said we needed to get to scale to win, will you come back and help me build it."*

I said yes and laid the groundwork in 2017 that would position us to be the central driving force of the 2018 Second Chances Florida Campaign, guaranteeing that returned citizens would lead the charge in an authentic and powerful way. Here is how we did it:

First, we built a foundation, setting-up systems for fiscal sponsorship, securing office space and hiring core staff. We completed a strategic planning process to develop organizational goals and created baseline administrative guidelines to achieve operational excellence.

Second, we pulled together the coalition with a Statewide Convening, bringing together 400 volunteers and dozens of national partners and funders. This event catapulted FRRC to a new level of funding capacity, entrenched our position in leading the ballot initiative work and resulted in a streamlined system for collective action around grassroots petition collection.

Third, we shaped the dominant narrative, working with our media firm, pollster and the grassroots communications committee to develop values-based messaging tools, then launched a full-scale effort to train partner organizations and volunteers on messaging discipline.

Fourth, we wrote a comprehensive grassroots plan, which anchored 200 organizations and 13,700 volunteers around a shared strategy and centralized infrastructure to harness and unleash the power of the grassroots movement.

Fifth, we brought in resources that we could control, aligning the funding community around investing in:

1. cross-organizational capacity building projects and early field work.
2. engagement of infrequent voters and non-voters in hardest hit communities and communities of color
3. innovation projects that leveraged technology and volunteer power to scale.
4. substantial operational funds to ensure the long-term sustainability of the FRRC.

We did all of this in nine months and achieved ballot placement (Amendment Four) after submitting to the State 1.1 million petition signatures from Florida voters.

After we qualified in January 2018, I transitioned to the Second Chances Florida Campaign as Voter Engagement Director, to build and lead the organizing team. Together, with grassroots coalition partners and volunteers, we made 11.2 million attempts to reach Florida voters and engaged 1.1 million of them in one-on-one conversations about Amendment Four. Our grass tops consulting team launched a massive paid media campaign targeting conservative voters, and through this layered approach, we won with 64% of the vote. On November 6, 2018, we enfranchised more people at once than any single initiative since women's suffrage. We had given ourselves and our fellows a second chance. With God, all things are possible.

Questions to Ponder

What type of second chances have you been given in your lifetime?

How has your own life experiences impacted the liberation and healing of others?

If you had all the power in the world, which areas of institutionalized oppression would you dismantle?

What internalized oppression do you struggle with today?

Author
Mila Al-Ayoubi
Principal of The Wheelhouse Project, LLC
Tampa, Florida

"You are more
powerful than
you know; you
are beautiful
just as you are."
Melissa Etheridge

God is My CEO

I am blessed to be a Membership and Sales Strategist, a consultant. People often ask if I work alone in my business. I get excited to share that I work alone, however, God is CEO of my business. Most everyone smiles and says is "that is so cool."

I'd like to share the story of how God became CEO of my business. I had an amazing 27-year career at MSU. I started working at the university when I was just 17 years old. God put amazing people on my path, people that believed in me and invested in my growth and development. I took a different path than many, I went for the career and job I wanted, without taking the college route. I have been entrepreneurial since I was a young girl and have been able to build the most amazing lifelong career. In my role as Director of Sales at the Kellogg Center, I had the most amazing experiences,

I could write a book on that alone. I know my career was not just luck, it was hard work, taking risks, long hours, and most recently realizing God always had a plan for me. As I built my career, I got married and divorced, and was a single Mom most of my son's life. While working long hours, I committed to breaking the stereotype of a single parent or "broken home." I was active in my son's school activities and we cherished quality time together at home. As I look back it's easy to see the "footprints" poem. Jesus was carrying me through many seasons of my life, always preparing me for more.

After 27 exciting years at the Kellogg Center, I retired from MSU. As I retired, I was offered a perfect next step position as VP of Sales for an organization in the sales and hospitality industry. During my work, I had to undergo major, life changing, spine surgery. I had my scoliosis corrected, resulting in most of my spine being fused, and two 14" metal rods and 30 screws. I had a lot of complications, but never let myself get down. I felt blessed to be alive and kept a positive attitude which helped with recovery. It was a long recovery. (I promise I'm getting to how God became CEO of my business.)

Following the surgery, I was off work for four months. I returned for three months, at part-time, and found I was not able to return full time, based on the demands of the work and weakness of my physical body. So, I had a talk with myself and said, "You have always wanted to, and knew you would, start a consulting business one day, well this is the time. Time to put your faith where your mouth is." I always spoke of my faith and trust in God. Now was the time to jump off and trust completely. Give up the steady paycheck and benefits.

It was a real lesson, that I didn't trust God on my own. He had to force me out of the steady, safe work environment, and He asked me to put my trust into action. I pray that I am learning to trust God first!

I believe that God spoke to me through my surgery.

So, I'm happy to share that nine years ago I started my consulting business. I knew the only way I could make it was to trust God 100% with this new venture. With God as my CEO this business has grown beyond my wildest dreams or plans. God directs my steps, opens doors, and puts me in front of people I can help. I work hard to obey. I view my work each day as a ministry in many ways. I reach people across the U.S. and Canada and speak openly of my faith and how it is the foundation of my business.

Owning your own business can be scary. Knowing there is no revenue coming in unless you generate it. And yet, I don't worry if the clients will keep coming or will I stay relevant. I don't ask, what if? I work hard, do what I know God asks me to do, take care of others, be a woman after God's heart, and He takes care of the rest.

Prayer is a constant in my day. I only make strategic decisions after consulting with my CEO (God).

Growing my business, walking on stage to present conference sessions to 400 people, before taking a new direction, I pray! Each year I take my work into new and exciting directions, directions I would never have dreamed of. God speaks clearly to me and shows me His plans. You might ask, "how do you know this is from God?" When I feel at peace with a decision or direction, I know it's from God. If He has placed it on my heart and then I receive confirming messages through multiple people, platforms, or methods, I know it's from God. Sometimes I get too busy, and the days might get more difficult. I immediately know I have stopped listening, watching, and seeing God's plan. I quickly bring myself back on track, every day is a gift.

When I look back through the years it's easy to see that God is Good, and He had plans for me all along.

My son is grown, with a beautiful wife and they have blessed me with two little girls that steal this Gigi's heart. Business is thriving and I am excited at the growth plans I have moving forward. Trusting God as my CEO for business and life is the only way for me. Period.

"Your worries often reveal where you trust God the least."

Questions to Ponder

Is God your CEO?

How are you living out God's plan for your life?

What part of your life are you holding back from God?

Is there a facet of your day that you can trust to Jesus?

Do you ask the Holy Spirit to be with you in my tough moments and in your happy moments?

Author
Shari Pash
Owner and Membership and Sales Strategist
Strategic Solutions for Growth
Lansing, Michigan

"Through hard work,
perseverance and a
faith in God, you can
live your dreams."

Ben Carson

Rise of the Underdog

So, I find it hard to talk about myself, ever since my conversion. I BECAME NEW, in the most literal form.

So, let me take you back a bit. I was the youngest of five children. My Dad abandoned us when I was five, which left my Mom forced to work three jobs, which meant, we didn't really see her much. That left my older brother Todd to take care of me while my Mom was out making ends meet.

My Dad was my first heart break. He let me down so many times as a girl, and I always found myself trying to get him to "see" me. This led me into "looking for love in all the wrong places" at a very young age. Seeking acceptance from anyone who would "see" me. I was not "groomed" to succeed. I was groomed to fail.

I was told as a young girl that I had better marry a rich man, because my looks were all I had going for me. So, I lived those words spoken to me. I was the underdog from the start.

When I entered high school, all the upper classman boys wanted to date me. So, I dated them. I lost my virginity at the age 15, and smoked marijuana for the first time all at the same age.

I spent the first 35 years of my life searching for love. Trying to fill that Jesus sized hole in my heart. And everything was about me. I was the most selfish person you would ever meet. I was diagnosed as a narcissist. I used to deny it, but looking back, that was me. I love to tell this story because it is evidence of the transforming power of Jesus Christ. I believe God hand picks misfits like myself. The underdogs so that He can be glorified.

I have written three books that tell my whole story, so I won't use this space to do that. But I do want to make sure that you see the transforming power of Jesus Christ and what happens when you say YES and go ALL IN.

In April 2006 my third husband Curt, who I am still married to today, was on the road selling cars. I was home pregnant with my fourth child. We were broke, busted and disgusted, in every way. Bankrupt, home in foreclosure, on food stamps, and well, our marriage was terrible. Curt was a full-blown sex addict and was living into that while on the road. I didn't find out about this until 2013, which was God's plan, because I was looking for any way out.

We ended up at Ginghamsburg church and I remember thinking, "I want to feel like those people." You know the ones, praising and worshipping with their hands up not caring what anyone thinks.

God hooked me up with my spiritual Mother, Carolyn Slaughter and I did whatever she told me to do, starting with spending time with Jesus in the word of God every day. I mean, it is my instruction manual and after being in it for the last 13 years, it is the best leadership book out there today.

I found fitness and decided at the age 35 with four kids to train and compete in a figure competition. During that eight-week span, I was a brand-new person. And I was ON FIRE for Jesus. And I started living for him. I have been on this personal development journey ever since and I think I am pretty awesome. Glory to God!

Since then we have built a multi-million-dollar business, working on another. I started a ministry, "Women at the Well Ministry." Yes, because that was me. Jesus met me at my lowest and I said, I am all in Jesus! I've been telling people about Jesus ever since.

I have brought many people to Jesus Christ, have baptized 10 people, which is the most amazing experience ever! My husband Curt has been redeemed! He is more that I could have ever dreamt up. He is the Godliest husband, father, leader of anyone I know. His path is so clear and how he takes tragedies and turns them into good blows my mind.

In June of 2013, I get a call at 6:30 am that my older brother Todd (the one who took care of me) had committed suicide. He made sure the job got done, shot gun…you get the picture.

I woke up one morning and realized I had PTSD. The Lord led me to Yoga, then to Holy Yoga which is a 501c3 ministry that uses Yoga to share Jesus with people and then to trauma sensitive yoga. We have been using these modalities at our retreats ever since. I even created an app so that people can have a safe experience with Christian meditation and Holy Yoga.

We are now working with an organization called "Oasis house" which is a nonprofit that is helping women who have escaped the sex trafficking trade, who need healing. They all have PTSD. God is so cool.

So, my heart is now really using my wealth to do what we are supposed to do, take care of the widows and orphans and the extreme poor and stamp out this modern-day slavery.

So, friends, what is stopping you from going ALL IN with Jesus? Here is a staggering statistic: 98% of the population end up dead or dead broke by the age of 65 living off government assistance. That leaves two percent of us out being Gods' hands and feet.

One thing that I KNOW…...there are many "church players" who go to church on Sunday to check it off their list, and maybe open their Bible, which I don't even see people doing this anymore. You are missing out on your inheritance that God died and suffered for. It's time to jump ALL IN. He needs you! Your life matters! It is not in YOUR power that you will do this, it is the Holy Spirit's power! That is how underdogs win!!

Questions to Ponder

If you were told that you have six months to live, how would you change how you are living your life now?

Why would you wait until you get a death sentence to get moving toward your dream?

Author
Rachel Tucker
Founder-Women at the Well Ministries
racheltucker.org
Troy, Ohio

Going Back to School: God's Plan for Me

I am so blessed to do the work that I do. There is no doubt this is God's plan for me. I am a therapist and I am honored and humbled that people allow me into the most intimate areas of their lives. I have always wanted to be a therapist, but I became overwhelmed with the schooling necessary for this vocation. Upon graduating from high school, I chose another path and instead went in to marketing and merchandising. Yet, the field of psychology continued to call me. Meanwhile, I married and worked in retail for a short time and then went on to have my children and chose to be a stay-home mom. I absolutely loved being a stay-home mom. I felt fulfilled in every way. The thought of going back to work or even back to school never even crossed my mind. I have often told people, jokingly that I could be very happy being a potted plant in the foyer. I am somewhat introverted and prefer one on one interaction to large gatherings.

123

Then my life changed, and a different path was set before me.

My sister, who was also my best friend, was diagnosed with a serious and debilitating disease and rather than drawing my family closer; it caused more dysfunction and distance. It was at this time that I sought out therapy for myself. During my time in therapy my sister passed away. I am grateful I was in therapy as I was going to need the support. It was also during this time that my therapist commented that I should consider becoming a therapist myself. She had planted a seed. She had even gone further than that by bringing me a university class schedule and application. I did not think there was any way I was going back to school. I had many reasons why it wasn't possible. I had not been in school for more than ten years and I didn't even know if I would be accepted, not to mention how I would pay for it. Well, I would soon find out that God had a plan for me. I still marvel to this day at his wondrous deeds.

I began to look into the process and quickly discovered I had an arduous task ahead of me. I needed to take three more classes in psychology before I could even apply to the graduate psychology program. This would not be easy. I was beginning to worry that I would spend money on the three classes only to not be accepted into the program. I also had to decide on a school to attend. I realize now how crazy it was of me to only apply to one school, but that's what I did! The first school I looked into was the same school I did my undergraduate work at. This made sense to me. I remember coming home after talking with the department head and going straight to bed crying. I felt hopeless and wondered what I had been thinking. The next day, I decided to call one more university before giving up. The phone call went well enough that I decided to go talk with the director of the program I was considering. By the grace of God, the interaction with him was completely different and I felt some hope. I soon found out however, that there would be many things required of me in the process of applying to the program. I still wasn't sure if this was a good idea and I prayed to God for some sign that this was indeed his will for me. I talked to God constantly, looking for some direction. One evening, God answered my prayers.

My father had passed away a couple of years before my sister passed away and one night my father visited me. Let me explain what I mean here by saying he "visited" me. I was asleep when he came to me, somewhat like a dream, but way more vivid and real. I still remember the visit just like it was yesterday. That is the difference between dreams and visits. Visits are not vague, but instead are rather clear. I remember him telling me that God had plans for me and that I was to continue in my efforts towards this new career. There were other signs, but I still wasn't convinced. Then, finally one day I was out for a run and I called out to God. I had so many fears and could not see how this could work. I wasn't even sure how I would pay for it, which was a huge obstacle.

When I returned home from my run, I received a phone call from an insurance company informing me they had been trying to reach me because I was the beneficiary of an inheritance. This was back before computer filing and they had not been able to locate the beneficiary card. They were about to turn the insurance benefits over to the state when someone discovered the beneficiary card stuck down below the other cards in the file cabinet. Nothing short of a miracle, the inheritance would be enough to pay for my degree! I was stunned and overwhelmed. I now had the means to pay for the program, but I wasn't sure I would be among those accepted into the program.

I had been away from school for many years and was not adept at using a computer. I opted to take the required GRE (Graduate Record Examination) using pencil and paper. However, on the day I arrived to take the exam, they informed me they were no longer offering this option and I would have to take the computer version. I was overcome with anxiety. I had no idea how to use the computer and had to take the tutorial before beginning the exam. It felt like I was swimming upstream throughout this entire process. Somehow, I managed to complete the exam and went home exhausted.

Over the next few weeks I provided the university with all the necessary paperwork for my application. Then I waited. I was shocked when I received notification that I had been selected for an in-person interview, meaning I had made the first cut! I was excited and nervous. Then, days before my interview, I threw my back out while picking up a napkin off the floor and was rendered immobile. I ended up in the emergency room hunched over in pain. I had many things to do to get ready for my interview, but I could not drive my car and I could barely stand up. Friends rallied around and helped me prepare. One friend took me to get my hair done while another took my things to the dry cleaners.

On the day of the interview my husband drove me and helped me walk to the building. I was in agony. When I arrived, I discovered the interview would be conducted by a panel of psychologists. I had expected to be interviewed by a single person. Somehow, I managed to get through it. I was more than surprised when I received notification that I was being invited back for a second and final interview. To my amazement I was accepted into the program.

A week before the program was to start, my husband drove me to the parking lot for a trial run so I would know where to park and what building to go into. The university was in an urban environment that I was unfamiliar with and I was a nervous wreck. When we arrived that day and pulled up to the parking lot attendant, my husband rolled down the window and asked the attendant, "What's your name and do you own this lot?" The gruff attendant answered that his name was Chicho, and yes, he does own the lot. My husband responded with, "I'd like to introduce you to my wife. She's the most precious person in my life. I need to know that you will take care of her when she parks in your parking lot." Chicho assured my husband that he would be watching for me when I started classes the following week.

Sure enough, with all the other obstacles I had encountered, on the first day of class when I pulled up to the parking lot, there was a long line of cars and the parking lot was full. Another obstacle. Panicking, I found Chicho. With tears in my eyes, I asked him if he remembered me and he said that he did. He told me that he would park my car and that I should just go off to class. With blind faith, I handed over my keys. Throughout that entire semester, Chicho not only valeted my car, he also cleaned the snow off it in the winter and always had my car ready for me. This gruff attendant was really a kind family man, who always enjoyed the baked goods I brought him and took me under his wing throughout the entire time I used that parking lot.

That was over 20 years ago, and I have never looked back. Personally, the decision to go down this path has been nothing short of a gift from God;

a calling. Before each patient comes into my office, I take a few minutes to pray for them and to ask the Holy Spirit to be present and allow God to use me as He wills in order to help this person. Along with drawing from my professional training, I incorporate spiritual reading and spending time with the Lord in order to provide guidance when working with my patients. This path has been at times emotionally difficult, but also gratifying. I am grateful that God has chosen me for this work and especially thankful that I stopped resisting and finally allowed myself to be led by the Holy Spirit down this path to do His will.

Questions to Ponder

Are you open to God's plan for you?

What are you willing to do to accomplish His Will in your life?

Do you know your heart's desire and does this align with God's Will for you?

Author
Anna Stapleton
Limited Licensed Psychologist
Canton, Michigan

"I think the reason I was successful is that I was never cynical."

Carol Burnett

WSW – Women Supporting Women

Butterfly Effect: The scientific theory that a single occurrence, no matter how small, can change the course of the universe forever.

I believe that every interaction is an opportunity. What if a chance encounter changed everything?

One said encounter, one serendipitous moment, is exactly why you are reading today. You see, it was a sunny Tuesday afternoon, I got on a plane from Orange County, CA destined to return to Detroit, Michigan. I sat next to Sr. Dorothy Ederer in row 22. THIS WAS NOT BY CHANCE, IT WAS FATE. As fate would have it, Dorothy was in the wrong row. She was given row 21. God sat us together with intention. We spoke for hours. During our less than chaotic four-hour flight we shared bits and pieces of our life with one another to pass the time. Who knew that "just passing the time" could create such a personal connection? Some personal connections are welcomed and encouraging. When I told her how many children I had and the group I started, "Women Supporting Women," she asked me if I would be willing to share how it all came about. Our conversation was a very pleasant one.

All interactions can be a vehicle for change and opportunity. Sometimes those interactions are an opportunity to reflect. I shared with her how group came about.

Six months earlier I had another chance encounter outside of a restaurant in New Orleans, Louisiana. This experience was 100% different, it would profoundly impact and forever change me. Let me first introduce myself and rewind to the backstory. I'm Carrie. I have four babies, my husband is a pilot and I am, well...I am ON 24/7. (for the most part) I am also an entrepreneur. In my early 20's I traveled the US dancing with a children's show. I loved living out of a suitcase, site seeing this great country of ours, so when I married a pilot and the roles were reversed, I was easily envious of his "lifestyle."

Years later, nine to be exact, I found out we were expecting our fourth child. I remember saying to him "you know who babysits four kids? NOBODY, that's who!" I had missed a few opportunities due to postpartum setbacks; I was NOT missing my

company's annual convention. Blaire was only eight months old and exclusively had to be nursed.
I made the bold decision to go and bring my baby.

The love and support I was given by my company and fellow executives were magical. High fives, pat on the back and "good for you" comments I received confirmed that I had made the right decision for my family and for myself. People were stopping me and asking if they could take our picture, because "this" is what dreaming bigger and grabbing life by the horns is all about.

I was feeling confident and empowered until that fateful evening while standing outside on Bourbon Street.

That night Blaire and I were invited to a huge celebration at Pat O'Brien's restaurant and at ten p.m. the whole establishment became a bar, at which point we left. I planned to take a ride home with a couple dear friends of mine who were finishing up sightseeing down Bourbon Street. My sweet baby girl was sleeping in her carrier and I was rocking her. It was 10:06 pm, I had just gotten off FaceTime call with my husband where I jokingly called myself "mother-of-the-year" for having our baby on Bourbon.

The universe must not have known I was kidding.

Seconds later a woman came charging at me from the bar across the street. The woman cussed me up one side and down the other about what a "bad mom" I was. I hate confrontation. It makes me very uncomfortable. It always has. I made sure that I looked her square in the eyes and said, "I see you and I hear you." I tried to explain but she continued scolding me, she got louder and louder, her response was alarming. She continued to call me "ridiculous." She was unwilling to hear anything I was saying and only willing to see the disturbing picture she had painted of the situation. I'm sure it was only a few minutes but at that moment it felt like an eternity. I was embarrassed and mortified. As I stood there, I reminded myself that I didn't know her journey or her story, after time and consideration I found peace.

The silver-lining is, I found my voice and a topic that ignites a fire deep down inside my soul. Finally, on October 3, 2018 I broke my silence and created a movement called #WSW on Facebook, standing for "Women Supporting Women."

Now we have a group of like-minded women that lift each other up within the group daily and at least once a week I go "live" and showcase someone or just talk about what is weighing on my heart now.

I will not be here on this earth forever, but my legacy will live on. My children and my children's children will forever be impacted by my actions NOW. I believe that character, a lot of times is a learned behavior. We are molds of the combination of the people who came before us, their actions and the lessons they have left behind. We usually pick up the values, habits and beliefs of those we associate with. What kind of example are we setting?

Questions to Ponder

What would you have done?

What would you have said?

What kind of legacy are you leaving?

How can we as women support one another?

Author
Carrie Kowalski, husband Mark and their four children Thomas, Amelia, Estele and Blaire
CEO of AIE
Founder of Women Supporting Women #WSW
St. Clair Shores, Michigan

"Power to me is the ability to make a change in a positive way."

Victoria Justice

A Life Not Planned

I am sitting in a village in a remote area of Timor Leste attempting to converse with the local people in a mix of English and Tetum. Despite feeling very uncomfortable and humble, I allow the children to follow their tradition of greeting teacher visitors by kissing their hand. I have come to this poor yet happy village as part of my work in setting up a partnership between a diocese in Australia and a parish community in Tibar, Timor Leste. I wish I could say that I had mapped my life out and that working in this area of Formation with staff and students is exactly what I had hoped to do but life isn't always so obvious.

I was born an only child to parents who instilled in me a good foundation of Catholic values. They were assisted by the Sisters of Charity who provided my education for 13 years and mom, dad and I were regular 7:30 am Sunday Mass goers at our local parish. My family tell me that from an early age they knew that I was going to be either a nurse or a teacher as my favorite pastime was subjecting my dolls to intricate operations or art lessons.

I made the choice to become a teacher and began my training in English and Visual Arts at a Catholic University. I also studied a course in Religious Education, not for any spiritual aspirations but solely because I thought it would give me a better chance of getting a job in a Catholic school, an environment that I was comfortable in.

It was during this time that I experienced a faith crisis. Since leaving school I found I began to lose interest in my own faith, and I became quite critical of the church. I began to see a big anomaly between what I called the real world and the relevance of my religion and church in my life. For quite a while I refused to go to mass much to the disdain of my parents. I think now that I was seeking out some sort of clarification and an understanding of what my purpose was. Perhaps I also craved a sense of belonging. I remember writing a letter to my Principal saying I can no longer teach Religious Education, so I did not teach religion for many years.

I met my husband in 1981, fell in love and married in 1984. My husband was a regular church goer and I returned to the church with him by my side.

In 1986 our first child was born. For me this was a pivotal moment and one I was craving. The moment he was born I had a sudden clarity of not only my place but a realization that something spiritual had happened to me and that it was not just connected to God, I was living it.

I returned to the classroom and I sought opportunities to assist the Religious Education Coordinator with his work. I used the tools I knew such as paint, drawing materials and even clay as a pathway for students to be more involved in their faith. What I didn't realize, at the time, was that I was using what I knew and what I loved to also nurture my own understanding of my faith. This thirst that I believe began here saw me return to study, a journey that has lasted for some twenty years including three master's degrees in the areas of Religious Education and Theology.

I gave birth to our second child in 1989. Another healthy son, but unfortunately a few weeks after his first birthday he passed away. He was born with a congenital disorder that had not been diagnosed.

Besides the shock, I remember feeling an emptiness like nothing I had ever experienced. My school community was at my door within hours. They grieved with us and organized the funeral. The Funeral Mass was a blur, but I remember standing in that church with my family and feeling the most intense love from the people around me. I realized then that what I was feeling was the strength and love of God.

In the coming years I was successful in becoming a religious education coordinator in three Catholic schools. Each of these roles were similar but each gave me new opportunities and new strengths. One gave me confidence and knowledge in the Catholic faith as well as insight into the whole concept of service within a community. Another gave me an experience and hunger for social justice, allowing me to tap into the faith of young people by running retreats and immersions and the realization that all things are connected to God. My last school allowed me to work more with staff and the school board in the area of formation which became my catchphrase 'formation is like the icing on the cake'.

And so, it brings me to my present role Teacher Educator-Formation. Leaving the classroom after 35 years to work with solely with teachers was a major decision. Teaching in the classroom was exhausting and sometimes challenging but it was also a privilege and joy and keeps one young and hungry for knowledge.

In reflecting holistically on the path that I have journeyed, there seems to be a logical direction and even a mapping that looks planned. I can honestly say that my journey has not been planned. Several doors that I thought I needed to be opened were closed and others I was going to disregard were opened. This has led me to understand two insights. Firstly, that our journey in life is connected to God. Secondly that it is in both the ordinary and the extraordinary that we can glimpse God: the paint, the holding and lose of a child, our daily work or a simple kiss on the hand by a village child. We don't need to plan it we just need to let it happen.

Questions to Ponder

Have you ever experienced a sense that God is present in your life? What did it feel like?

In reflecting on your life so far is there a direction or plan that has eneabled you to be where and what you are today? Can you see any connections to God?

Your relationships, work and events in your life impact who we are. How has one challenging event made you stronger?

Author
Donna Dempsey
Diocesan Teacher Educator-Formation
Sydney, Australia

"Listen to the murmur of water and you'll hear Mother Nature.
Listen to the stillness beneath, and there you'll find God."

Donald L. Hicks

Fetch Threads:
A Business Born of Infertility

The year was roughly 1992. I remember announcing from the backseat of our family van, "Mom, what if I don't want to be a nun?!" My mom responded with a laugh, "Why would you think you would have to be a nun?" All eight years of myself responded, "Well, all the saints were nuns, so if I want to be a saint, then I have to be a nun." She kindly responded, "You can be a saint without being a nun." She probably continued on about how we are all called to be saints, etc., but by then I had already received my answer: I didn't have to be a nun. This was important to me because it was as early as eight years old that I felt the call on my heart to be a mom.

It will come as no surprise then that my favorite childhood toy was my baby doll. I have three brothers and asserted myself as their second mother from a young age. I started baby-sitting at 11 yrs old and by the time I graduated high school,

I had baby-sat for pretty much a relation of everyone in our small southwest Michigan town. I loved to see how others "did life." It was such a beautiful gift to be invited into the homes of families I befriended as my very own and learn how they made everything work. I did their laundry, cleaned their homes, fed, and played with their children. I was a mother-in-training.

In college I had thought I met my match. He was a wonderful man and my first love. There was no doubt in my mind he would make a great father. I just knew we would get married someday. The summer after I graduated from college, we hit the uncertain terrain of establishing ourselves in careers and relocating. Our relationship didn't survive. I was devastated. It was about nine months later that I began dating another man I was convinced was going to be my husband. He was wonderful and valued me in so many ways. I fell for him, hard. He would often affirm me and say, "You're going to be a wonderful mother someday." As we got deeper and deeper into our relationship, his own uncertainties came up. He expressed uncertainties around marriage and children. He wasn't sure he wanted marriage and children. Um, what? Did he know who he was with? Unfortunately, he did, and I learned the hard way that even my love couldn't heal his fears inside.

It took me a long time to heal from that last relationship, but without the time spent in it, I would never have met my husband at the perfect time. The person I married is a wonderful human being. We share many things, among them, our values and a shared vision of family. We began trying to have a baby 6 months after we got married. We got pregnant very quickly and couldn't believe our luck. We sat in the smug seat of just believing that we had "done everything right" in order to conceive (and fast). It was at the elective 12 week ultrasound that we heard the most earth-shattering words: "there's no heartbeat." Our worlds came crashing down around us.

The months that followed our miscarriage were spent doing everything we could to grieve and move forward. We heard stories upon stories of people who got pregnant six weeks following their miscarriage or very quickly thereafter. Two years later, I can say that isn't our story. In fact, I spent the greater part of those years resisting our story: infertility. How was this possible? We went from OB to Reproductive Endocrinologist. From acupuncturist to chiropractor. At this point it would be a shorter list to state what we haven't done in order to conceive.

A friend recently shared something a woman said about her own infertility journey: "we need to lift the veil of shame and secrecy." That very line cuts to the core of my experience.

I never considered the amount of shame infertility had caused me. Shame that I wasn't doing enough, that somehow this was my fault and within my control. No one is ashamed of a cancer diagnosis or learning of their diabetic condition. Why is reproductive health so different? What works for one person in achieving pregnancy may not work for another. Bodies are so individual and the joining of two pools of DNA is complex. Even within the same families there is such variety, how would we think that arriving there would be any different?

There is also the added spiritual layer of shame. Maybe it's because we refer to babies as a blessing (and they are certainly a gift), but what does that language mean for the one who is not conceiving? For the one who doesn't have a baby in her arms? Unblessed? No. That's just not true and it's sloppy theology to say God decides who gets pregnant. As Fr. Greg Boyle says, "God is too busy loving us to desire a particular outcome." The God I know wants the fulfillment of the desires of our hearts. The God I know invites me to live the paschal mystery -- the hope of resurrection in the midst of cycles of constant grief and heartbreak of infertility. The God I know says, "watch what I'm going to make of this mess."

This has been the hardest season of my life. My past devastating breakups don't compare, the depression and anxiety that ramped up in college and into my adult life don't compare. Infertility hits to the core of my identity and who I know God is calling me to be. I haven't stopped pursuing this path, and the thing is, God has shown up. God's shown up in the sweet and silly persona of our golden retriever puppy, born of infertility. God has shown up in the faces of the community of women who have come forward and said, "You're not alone." God has shown up in the quiet nudges that lead me to pursue others things in this space. One of those nudges was in an arena that I find incredible delight and enjoyment: shopping.

I have a passion for deals and love to shop specifically for kids' clothes. My background is in child development and I feel strongly that kids' clothes can be cute and practical. I value sustainability and have an eye for second-hand designer gems as well as brand new discounts. I believe confidence starts with how you feel. Also, I love the hunt and I LOVE a good deal! As a child, my emotions were often linked to what I was wearing. My earliest childhood memories become clearer when I recall the outfit that I had on. My dad would always joke with me when I would recall a story that happened in my childhood and would ask, "And what were you wearing?"

My business, "Fetch Threads" was born out of the ongoing requests I would get to assist friends and relatives to find the perfect clothes for certain occasions. People would often tell me, "you could go into business!" So finally, I did.

It was my way of taking back something that infertility had stolen from me – the desire to surround myself with things that reminded me of children. It makes me happy to see kids so excited about their new clothes, and I love that I can use my gifts and talents to give families something so essential back to their lives: time.

I can't say that it all makes sense right now, but God has proven faithful and the fruit of generating life is happening all around, even if it's not in the form of baby, yet.

Questions to Ponder

How is God weaving your stories together?

What is a surprise that was unwelcome at the time, but has later born fruit?

Author
Andrea Rentz
Child Life Specialist and Personal Shopper for Kids Clothes
myfetchthreads.com
Ann Arbor, Michigan

A Mom, A Daughter, Two Men and a Truck

I was a first-generation graduate from Central Michigan University in 1984. I always worked growing up and through school. I worked in retail, as a waitress, a bartender, even a magician's assistant! I've always enjoyed working, making money which meant independence, and serving others.

Soon after college I moved to Atlanta, Georgia with a couple of waitress friends. I mainly moved to avoid the recession that was hitting Michigan especially hard. I was in search of opportunity. In Atlanta I had several various jobs, I waitressed, bartended, sold mainframe computers, sold air conditioners on the phone, got my Real Estate license and sold real estate, was a food broker and finally got the career job of my dreams, as a pharmaceutical sales representative. I learned so much from this job, actually all my jobs!! This opportunity also helped me pay off my share of student loans, get out of debt and actually start saving money which is so empowering.

In 1987 I started a **Two Men and a Truck** business at my mom's urging. I went out and bought an old used truck as she did and painted **Two Men and a Truck** on the side. I ran the business from my apartment and parked the trucks at a small Baptist church across the street. I asked if I could pay them? They said, "no, but we will be praying for your success." I did not attend this church; their generosity truly touched my heart. I kept my "real" job in pharmaceutical sales, as I viewed this moving business as more of a hobby. In 1989 my Mom franchised the business and I became her first Franchisee!

In the early 1990's I started getting homesick, so I moved to Novi, in the Detroit area. I got a new pharmaceutical sales job and started another **Two Men and a Truck** franchise. Again, I ran the business from my apartment and this time parked the trucks behind the Novi Bowling Alley.They DID want me to pay to park my trucks there!

In March of 1994 my mom asked me to be President of **Two Men and a Truck/USA** (we have since renamed it **Two Men and a Truck/ International).** She wanted me to take over while she pursued a career in politics. At the time we had one part time person in the office, my mother and I didn't take a salary for a few years as the franchise company couldn't afford to pay us. I accepted the offer and finally quit my pharmaceutical sales job and relied on my **Two Men and a Truck** franchise to pay my bills! I think the other franchises appreciated that I no longer treated my franchises like a hobby on the side. It continued to grow and do well.

I think the reason for our success at all the franchise locations, then and now, is that my mom instilled the value and belief to always take good care of our customers. I followed my mom's footsteps in three other ways as well.Take care of your staff, your community and market whenever possible. Back then all we could afford to do was leave business cards everywhere!! This was before the internet and we couldn't afford the big fancy yellow page ads back then.

Like any new business, we ran into our share of obstacles in those early years. Because there was no Internet, I had no way to research franchising and I did not understand how this business model worked. I knew how to run my franchise but not the franchise company. There weren't even any franchising books at the time. God blessed us countless times along the way.

We thankfully won a grant from the state of Michigan paying for one year of free consulting services from Deloitte and Touche. I met with our consultant every Tuesday for a year! He pointed out that we were not charging enough for our services. We increased our royalty payments from 4% to 6%. This helped us significantly, we could now afford to start hiring people. He also persuaded us to come up with a Mission Statement. I was reading the book, *Good to Great* at the time and was inspired to work on our Core Values, values that Mary Ellen instilled from day one. These values guide **Two Men and a Truck** to this day.

At my mother's persuasion we also joined the International Franchise Association. The people we met and the best practice lessons we learned from other franchise companies is absolutely priceless. I went on to become the third female board chair in the Association's 55-year history. An absolute honor but challenging.

When I took over as President of **Two Men and a Truck** I had the honor and opportunity of fine-tuning paperwork, training materials, and marketing pieces. Everything was built upon what my mom had established. I implemented the many ideas I learned from pharmaceutical sales and the many other jobs I had held. At **Two Men and a Truck**, the evolution of how things are done never stops.

Over the years **Two Men and a Truck** continues to grow and prosper. In the early years at my mother's persuasion, she suggested we give 10 cents from every move to a national charity. For many, many years we gave to the American Cancer Society, hundreds of thousands of dollars. Today our national charity is called Convoy of Hope.

In 2007, my title changed from CEO to board chair. My brother, Brig Sorber,took on the position of CEO. I was able to dedicate my time to the International Franchise Association and to my family.

My husband survived cancer during my **Two Men and a Truck** journey. We were blessed by twin sons after trying in-vitrothree times. Now our boys are graduating college, my husband Noel of almost 25 years continues to be my greatest supporter

(Noel and my mom have always supported me 100%).

Today we have almost 200 people in our home office, hundreds of franchisees in four countries and over 1,800 trucks on the road. Who would have thought? I give God all the credit.

My title remains chair of the board. I spend my time volunteering, mainly for hospice, and I'm on a nonprofit board for a home for the mentally challenged called Chosen Vision.

This journey has been amazing beyond anything I ever could have dreamed. There are many success stories within **Two Men and a Truck**, many movers went on to become very successful franchisees.

The amazing thing to me is that over the years and many types of executive leadership, our mission and core values have remained unchanged and true. They are practiced from the top down, bottom up and sideways! They are a part of our awards programs, strategic planning, hiring, evaluations. Our core values have essentially become our culture.

The mission statement did come first and that is, **Two Men and a Truck** strives to "exceed customer expectations in value and provided a high standard of satisfaction."

Our core values are: care, give back to the community, be people of integrity, and treat others as if they were your grandma.

At the end of the day I believe in: diversity, to be your best and have fun, work hard, love lots, give thanks, give back and never get too big for your britches.

Question to Ponder

What is the purpose of a business giving back with time and/or treasure?

Author
Melanie Lyn Bergeron
Chair of the Board
Two Men and a Truck International
Okemos, Michigan

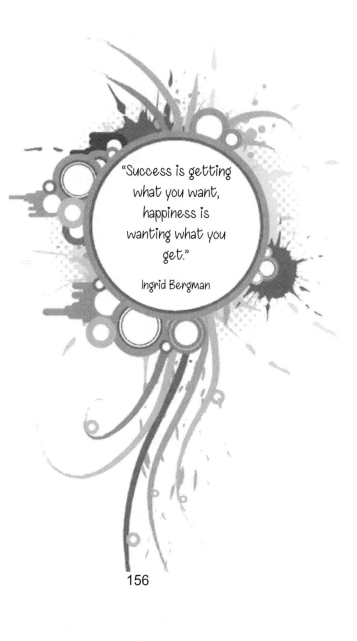

"Success is getting what you want, happiness is wanting what you get."

Ingrid Bergman

God is Everywhere, Even in Your Closet

Each new day holds the promise of endless possibilities. I could never have imagined how my life would change on November 18, 2017. It was one of those gorgeous fall days when the sun was shining, the air was crisp and the leaves shone in an array of warm colors. While taking in that beauty, a man suddenly pulled out in front of me after running through a stop sign and I was violently rear-ended. Thankfully, no one was hurt. The man who hit me totaled his work truck but believe it or not my car barely had a scratch. That in of itself seemed pretty miraculous and totally validated the safety rating of my vehicle. As I was driving home, despite feeling shaken, this immense feeling of gratitude and love consumed me. I know now that God was with me, and of course, He always is. On that same drive home, my friend Leigh Ann called me. She was a new friend to me and had probably only called me a handful of times prior, so I happily took her call. Upon asking me what I was up to, I explained that I had just been in a minor car accident. She seemed a little reluctant to explain why she was calling but I assured her that I was fine and happy to hear from her. At that moment, she said something that completely changed the trajectory of my life.

"Sara, you are going to think I'm crazy, but this morning, when I was in my closet, the Holy Spirit told me to call you."

Whoa. Ok…I'm listening…I mean, that is not the type of phone call I receive every day! She went on to explain that she wanted to make galoshes like her grandfather used to wear, only cuter and for women. She had planned that evening to attend the MSU Men's Basketball game and even though it was gorgeous weather at that moment, the forecast suggested the weather would turn to sleet and freezing rain. Drastic weather changes are a way of life for Michiganders and something we tend to just accept. Now, Leigh Ann is from the south and although she had been living in Michigan for about ten years, she was very frustrated by the way the weather dictated her fashion choices. She had picked out some great suede booties to wear that evening and realized that now she had to figure out a new outfit and shoe selection. As I listened, my heart swelled with joy as she told me about her desire to create this amazing product. Even more amazing, I explained to her, was that I had the perfect name for our company *Patten.*

About a year prior to that day, I was trying to create shoes that were not only cute, but also comfortable. My husband's cousin, Tom, and I worked on this project as he had some background working with manufacturers in the footwear industry. We brainstormed many names for our potential company and one we really liked evolved as we thought about our dads–Pat and Tom– both of whom died from cancer too young. We each had such a strong connection to our dads and hoped we might find a way to honor them in our work. So, Pat and Tom kind of morphed into Patten. Well, upon some research, we discovered that Patten was the name for a protective shoe cover in the middle ages. It seemed ironic that the name was related to footwear, but it wasn't quite right for what we were doing at *that* time. Due to many circumstances, Tom and I decided to put that shoe project on hold. Leigh Ann was aware of this venture and had asked me about it a week or so before the day the Holy Spirit reached out to her. I told her that it I was no longer working on it, but I just couldn't really let it go. When she called me on that fateful day, *Patten* really started making a lot of sense.

After that day, *Patten* quickly took shape. Leigh Ann and I found out very early on that we were great partners and had not only the desire, but the commitment to see this through. Tom, my partner in the shoe project, also signed on as a minority partner to help us get up and running. We made so many amazing connections in that first year and worked tirelessly to put a small company together. Through all of this, it was abundantly clear that God was in the center of everything we did! During this time, we were astonished and blessed by how we kept connecting with the right person for whatever our next step was. There were so many times God showed up for us that we started documenting our experiences. If we ever question why we are doing this, we can just go back to this ever-evolving list and find the strength to carry on.

Just one day shy of a year later November 17, 2018, we launched *Patten*. The MSU Women's Basketball coach, Suzy Merchant, graciously offered to host our launch party at her beautiful home. We really didn't know what to expect or if anyone would show up but the turnout and support, we received was incredible. The local news came, we had a fashion show, and Coach Merchant talked to the attendees about her passion for helping young women. We signed on to be a sponsor for her leadership retreat for girls called *empowHER*. Since our launch we have been able to contribute a few thousand dollars to her organization and grow our business. We started with four weather-related products including an umbrella, scarf, gloves and a raincoat. Over the next year and a half, we expanded our weather-related offerings and have enjoyed many unique opportunities. We are currently very close to launching the *Patten* – the shoe cover idea that brought us together. It's an exciting time and one that finds us leaning on God more than ever to show us the way. We have come far but we have so much more work to do and I have no doubt He will be with us.

Since *Patten's* inception, we have been committed to giving back to others in our community. In addition to our sponsorship of empowHER, we have also been able to help young girls and women by donating some of our products to them. Recently, we had several beautiful winter coats that we wanted to pass along to some women in need. We intended to donate them to an organization we work with regularly, but it had not yet worked in my schedule to drop them off. One evening, Sister Dorothy was at our home for dinner and she was speaking about the women she counsels and the challenges they face in their lives. It became clear to me that those women were the ones who would benefit from receiving the coats. God's timing is always right, and I trust he had me hanging on to those coats until that evening. It is truly an honor to be able to help those around us and as *Patten* grows, we intend to continue this tradition of giving on a much larger scale.

When I reflect on this journey, what I see the most clearly is how my faith has grown and my relationship with God continues to develop. Leigh Ann has been a great mentor to me because she has cultivated her relationship with Jesus in a way I had not really considered. I was raised in the Catholic church and have always felt close to God in my own way, but I didn't take time every day to talk to God or dream with Him. Recently, Leigh Ann purchased a daily devotional for me. I had dabbled with devotionals in the past but never really made a commitment to read it daily. She taught me that all the cool Bible study people highlight and write in their devotionals. So now, every morning, I get pretty excited to get out my colorful pens and highlighters and go to town marking up my devotional.

Co-creating *Patten* with God and trusted friends has been the spiritual journey of a lifetime. From the outset, I did not anticipate that divine intervention would be the highlight of this experience but that's exactly what it has become. I have learned that with God, all things are truly possible. Anxiety, fear and worry creep in when we leave God behind. All too often, we forget this truth and try to figure it all out on our own. That's a lonely place to be and I am thankful that this opportunity proved to me that God is always with us and God wants us to find success and abundance in all facets of our lives. All we need to do is keep listening because we never know when God will speak to us. As we learned, it very well might be in those quiet moments in our closet. I'm incredibly grateful to have been married to Scott for 15 years. He has always encouraged and supported me to follow my dreams.

Questions to Ponder

Can you think of a time in your life when the Holy Spirit came to you in an unexpected way or place?

In what ways could you strengthen your personal relationship with God?

Is God a part of your problem-solving process?

If not, how might you invite Him to help you when you are unsure of the next step to take?

Authors
Sara Gillespie
Husband: Scott; Children: Scotty and Sophie
Company *Patten*
East Lansing, Michigan

"Real generosity is
doing something
nice for someone
who will never find
out."

Frank A. Clark

Moments of Grace

One could say that I followed a rather conventional path in starting my own business; I completed formal education, entered a career in education that spanned for more than 20 years, and then quietly opened my own consulting firm. But looking a little deeper, I now see this journey as filled with synchronous moments replete with grace and love.

As a young girl growing up in Texas, I was always intrigued with the idea of being a business owner. My grandmother ran a small grocery store, which was smack in the middle of a growing community and my father owned his automotive business. At first glance, the life was not glamorous; our days started early and ended late and in between filled with the hustle and bustle of buying and selling. There were marketing activities going on all the time while we somehow simultaneously and automatically served our clients. We worked hard and always gave our best. Yet, on the flip side, all the hard work and energy did not guarantee sales or steady enough flow of cash to create a sense of peace. Looking back, I am in awe of how hard working my family was and how dedicated they were in ensuring that there was always food on the table and a roof over our heads.

My family tried to discourag me from starting my own business; they said it was not all that it is cut out to be and times would be difficult. Instead I was encouraged to go to college find a job with a stable income and a "safe" way of living. It was the traditional advice from parents: "Go to school to get a degree and get a good job." And so, I did.

During my first years in my profession, I knew I had entrepreneurial blood. I constantly sought out opportunities to create and design. I wanted to serve others in a not very predictable manner, thinking of what customers needed rather than what I preferred to give them. I enjoyed the speed of the business world and read everything new in the literature.

At one point of my career, I led a community college division, corporate and community development, and I fell in love with it. I was responsible for designing and creating programs, connecting with the community and building partnerships. It was hugely different from teaching in a classroom. I grew quickly into the corporate mindset and felt ever so alive. The experience of these human-centered moments was life-giving and filled me with exciting insights into grace and gratitude. From the day-to-day grind of early family struggles, I blossomed into the creativity of gratitude, wherein being grateful for new opportunities, I came to launch new approaches to helping others. I began to understand that our work impacted the lives of others in unique ways and for the first time in my "traditional education" career I heard my calling.

However, along the way, I was cautioned by mentors and friends that I should follow a slower and more traditional path. I was often told that community and business needs were constantly changing and this would not be good for my career. Advisedly, my career was supposed to move in a more predictable progression.

Toward the end of my last traditional job, I found myself searching for a "deeper calling" and when faced with the opportunity to move to another state for another position in the same traditional educational setting, my head and heart simply said NO! Although, I was not sure of the future, I felt I must be true to my vision and my gifts. I was eager to create and design solutions, which were human-centric and could impact people. With helping people and organizations grow, I would experience moments of grace.

So, with the help of my loving husband and my faith in God, I redirected my life and opened a new consulting firm, Strategies by Design. I am passionate about helping people feel alive at work while providing services, creating products or solutions with the peoplr we serve as the foundation of all our actions. Our organization is dedicated to helping leaders, teams, and organizations design services and experiences in a human-centric manner. We help teams become more vibrant and aligned while ensuring every voice is heard and honored. Let me give you a quick example, I recently worked with a small but very friendly team in helping them create a stronger alliance with each other and the people they serve. After spending an hour or so with them I found that some people were more extroverted while others sat quietly during our conversation.

I knew everyone was on board, had an opinion or a story to share, but somehow did those voices ever get heard. My mind quickly filled with thoughts and questions. What if this is the same for serving clients. Is it possible, this team like so many others, respond to the loudest voice? I searched for a different approach to how we lead people and teams.

During one of my moments of grace, I picked up a book at an airport called, *Change by Design: How Design Thinking Transforms Organizations and Inspires Innovation* (2009) by Tim Brown.

This book spoke to my heart, my mind, my soul. The book spoke of the genius within each of us and called us to design a new approach to serving others, in a human-centric manner. I was now hooked and so my business was designed with a purpose.

Looking back at my life, my journey has been filled with moments of grace all woven into a unique tapestry. I am in awe of God's amazing love for me and his gentle hand on my journey.

In retrospect, I can now connect the dots of how divine Providence led me through a "traditional educational career" to the creative service enterprise I am presently in.The grace of it all has shown me that steady gratitude of heart reveals the secrets of creativity and innovation in the service of others.

Questions to Ponder

Reflecting on your present work, are you at the level of satisfaction you have been seeking?

At the end of each day, do you experience a sense of gratitude for the events of the day?

Do you have an awareness of God's providence in your journey of life?

Author
Judith Cardenas, Ph.D.
Husband: Bernie
Judith@strategiesbydesigngroup.com
strategiesbydesigngroup.com
East Lansing, Michigan

My Child...
One Person at a Time

Am I making a difference? I think so? I hope so?
Am I leaving my mark on this world? Well from
what Google says about the women who are
making a difference it is a HARD NO for me. These
women I have read about are doing rallies,
marches, legislative changes, speaking
engagements, documentaries, massive protests,
are CEO's and so much more.

Wait...God just stepped in.

I click on a random YouTube Link from BuzzFeed
as I am googling "Women Making a Difference."
As I am intently watching I realize that I have done
makeup on one of these seven women in this
video. While working on *The Late Show with
Stephen Colbert* I did Jacinda Ardern, Prime

Minister of New Zealand's makeup for her appearance. WOW. Out of all the videos, out of all the powerful women in the world, and links I could have clicked on, I clicked that one. Hi God, I said to myself with a smirk, and my God winked.

That was a quick and for me laughable reminder that EVERY SINGLE PERSON makes a difference. I am not famous, nor do I have to be to make a difference. I do not have millions of followers on social media, nor do I have too. Yet whatever I do, I do it with all my heart and people feel that, that is what makes all the difference. And maybe just maybe, my heart, character, work ethic, words of encouragement, faith, smile and genuine attitude towards others has individually impacted each person I encounter... making a difference.

I am one of five full-time makeup artists on America's number one morning show *Good Morning America.* This is not by talent alone. There are tens of thousands of makeup artists in the New York City area and some are more talented than I. Yet, God chose to place me there. Being in the presence of the women I work with, from the anchors to celebrities, life coaches, correspondents, guests, crew, friends of friends, most of these women have made a difference in my life without even knowing it. One person at a time.

I listen to their guidance on careers, money management, IRA's, loans, taxes, health, exercise, food and more. This makes a huge difference in my life and they do not know what I receive from them and apply in my life.

In February of 2008, I was 23 years old. I had routine blood work done in preparation for surgery for a breast augmentation. I found out my white blood cells were trying to take over my body. Thank you God for this mandatory blood work, because I never would have had a random blood check, especially not in my prime years at the young age of 23. But having a life-threatening disease in your twenties carries a special set of challenges both psychologically and socially that I was not even thinking about .

My parents were the ones who told me. They came into my bedroom shaking and holding back tears. I did not cry, I had to be strong for them. My initial reaction was shock, I went silent and after a few seconds of disbelief I hugged my parents and let them know that "its ok I'd rather it be me than my sisters or you."

I meant this. You see, I am a believer. I am a fighter. I am strong willed. I have listened to Joel Osteen enough to know that I was going to fight and win this battle with my thoughts, spoken words, and a positive attitude. This was not going to take my life especially because I am only 23! God has so many promises that have not been fulfilled for me yet! I knew this was going to be a long season, I had to fight both physically and mentally. However for me, it was more mentally and I was already prepared for battle and I WILL WIN.

I realized early that age is an inescapable part of how we view life moving forward and effects the decisions we make. All I wanted to do was cling to my family and career. I changed. Family time became my most valued time and I dove into my career with determination.

We all have a story. While walking your own path to life- positive, negative, promotions and failures, all these work together for your good, in God's timing. Stay on your path. Have short term goals to accomplish your long term vision. Preparation is the entranceway to walking, not running,to your destination. Enjoy the process and you will look back and thank God later. Character is your key to unlocking doors when preparation and opportunity meet. Success is what fills the room.

At 30 God winked again. This time through my wonderful mother and her direct prayers. "Lisa I just met with a girl and she is placing her baby up for adoption. Would you want to adopt?" Without thinking I said "of course I would." It was the only thought that came to my mind then and throughout the whole process, which was seven months. My mom prayed and asked God to let me adopt this child because she was worried about me stopping my daily medication which was keeping me in remission. I knew Motherhood was to be a part of my life, and heart, but I thought when I planned it. I was single, 30, and blooming in my career but my God had actually bigger plans. I knew this was God ordained and that he had great plans for this child's life.

I embraced this next chapter without question and opened my heart to whatever God planned. Little did I know how much the birth and growth of my daughter would completely hit the reset button on my life in the utmost beautiful way possible. I live each day with a sense of gratefulness and true thankfulness. I never fully understood what that meant until my daughter and I felt the power of living life with this energy.

To my daugher: I only can pray that I can be all God has created me to be in this life for you. The difference you have made in my life thus far has taught me loving lessons deep within my soul that only you could have delivered. You, my babe, are more of a blessing everyday than I could ever have imagined possible, and I think big. Olivia Harper Hayes from the day you were born, you became my sunshine and reason to live. My child… one person at a time.

Questions to Ponder

What do you think God is asking of you?

Have you had situations in your life that called forth your faith to be stronger in God?

Are you working each day to be all that God has called you to be?

Author
Lisa Hayes, daughter Olivia Harper
Good Morning America Make Up Artist
Long Island, New York

Seek God's Hand in Everything

High school is a time of uncertainty, insecurity, and loneliness, when many young people feel that they will never fit in the way that they are. It is a time when everyone feels so different from one another, yet they are all similar in their feelings. I think it takes years of experience to realize that we are all more the same than we are different–that God made all humans to desire the same things: love, acceptance and companionship. As a woman who has already turned the page on her high school years, I do not look back on them as fondly as I would like.I wish it had been easier for me to be genuinely myself, the woman God made me to be. However, the truth is that this will never be an easy feat and that the uncertainty does not magically dissipate when you walk across the stage at graduation.

While this might be the truth of after life, some women with incredible faith in God have been working to create a community that provides young women a place where they can be their genuine selves and develop a relationship with their creator, even in the depths of their high school hallways.

Adopted from Colossians 2:2-3, *building a community encouraged in heart and united in love* is the mission statement of this high school women's community, *Redefine 9*.

Redefine 9 is a spiritual beacon for all high school women, regardless of their school affiliation or faith background. Families of the girls in the group open their homes to us, where we can meet new friends, catch up with old ones, laugh, and learn about Jesus Christ. We have welcomed those who have grown up solidly in the faith—many of whom end up on our leadership team—as well as those who have never even heard the gospel, which usually turns out to be the coolest stories to tell. Social time at our meetings feeds into talks and testimonies from our college leaders and guest speakers, and concludes with small group discussion questions about the talks. While *Redefine 9* currently meets as a group twice a month, it has recently brought us immense joy that many girls want to meet more often to delve deeper into their faiths.

After being part of the *Redefine 9* community during high school and serving on our leadership team,

I was passed the baton and began leading the group during my sophomore year of college. As I enter my junior year, I am continuing to coordinate our meetings. We have increased the number of times that we meet and I am working hard to bring more girls into the group and a relationship with Jesus. It is truly amazing, and even chilling sometimes, to hear these young women talk about God and about their faith, and to witness the curiosity of women who have never experienced God's love like this before.

My favorite moment in my time so far has been the Holy Spirit urging a junior girl, whose family does not attend church regularly, to begin a summer bible study with her friends. It is moments like these that keep me passionate about our mission, even when meeting attendance may be low or when we haven't seen a new face in a while. Even in the difficult times when it seems like we are not reaching the girls as we would have hoped, God always reminds us why we are here and how far we have come.

The group was founded in 2015 by a friend of mine named Claire Conzelman during her junior year at Saline High School, when she found herself discontent with the lack of faith of her peers and the surroundings at school. On the verge of disenrolling from Saline High, she and her mentor, Kristin

Dolsen, a mother of three Saline graduates, spearheaded *Redefine 9*. They began by contacting all the young Christian women who they thought would form a strong foundation for their dream. Kristin and Claire both worked hard to make their vision come to life. I am eternally grateful that I was one of the women that they invited to embark on this spiritual journey to bring young high school girls to Jesus.

Another woman who was called to serve in the group is one of my current mentors, Shaina Sondakh, who guided the group of us young women tirelessly until her college graduation. Her faith in God, dedication to us, and selflessness in service showed me who God wanted me to be, and she became my role model (she would be embarrassed to hear me talking her up like this).

Without these women, I would not be where I am today, nor would a group such as *Redefine 9* likely exist at all. But I cannot forget the most powerful driving force of these blessings: God has taken the reins of *Redefine 9* and shown us in times of both prosperity and strife, that He has complete control over the hearts of everyone that our group touches. He has proven that nothing is more powerful than His word and spirit in bringing people to Him. Through my position in *Redefine 9*, God has taught me that even when I do not see it, His hand is in everything, guiding us on the path He has already paved for us. I cannot wait to see how many more young women He touches with the gift of *Redefine 9.*

In my experiences both in *Redefine 9* and elsewhere, I have realized how easy it is to be prideful. I will be the first to admit that I have sometimes forgotten that all of my skills and gifts are from God alone and not from myself or my experiences. In my life, I tend to be unnecessarily hard on myself and to take tasks upon my own shoulders when I feel like I am not doing enough. It has taken time for me to truly see God's hand in every situation where I believed I had accomplished triumphs on my own or had failed because of my "lack" of skill. God has tugged on my heart long and hard to tell me that He has guided every moment on my timeline and has placed or removed every person necessary in each point of growth. It is impossible for me to think back on my time in *Redefine 9* and not remember the women that came before me, who made *Redefine 9* happen every week and who exhibited the exact person that I wanted to be one day. Claire, Kristin, and Shaina were placed strategically in my life by the One who knows me best and were all significant parts of my journey. They have taught me to trust God always and to seek His hand in everything.

Questions to Ponder

Who in your life has God strategically placed on your path to bring you closer to Him?

How can you be a mentor and pathway for others that may be seeking God through you?

Author
Gillian Hartley
Student at the University of Michigan
Leader of *Redefine 9*
Saline, Michigan

Found by Love

My story is about a little girl who was lost and longed to be found by love. And God, in His great mercy, at just the right time, found her. As you read my story, may you hear the story of God's pursuing, faithful, and unconditional love.

My parents married very young. At age 21, my mom had three children and an alcoholic husband. As a little girl, I was troubled by the fighting between my parents. I was overwhelmed by fear, especially the fear that my parents would divorce. I so wanted to live a "happily ever after" life, but I knew in my young heart that things weren't right. I began to wonder whether I was part of the problem, whether I was good enough and whether I was worthy to be loved.

I began to try to earn the love of my parents and others. I tried to be what I thought people wanted me to be.

The tension grew in our home and I was always wondering whether the bottom of my world was going to drop. It dropped in 1979 when my older brother, Tom, killed himself at the age of 19. I was 16 and a senior in high school. My younger brother, Tim, was 14.

My dad blamed himself and my mom couldn't handle the loss. Within months she was addicted to prescription drugs and drinking heavily. Unlike my dad, my mom was not a functioning alcoholic. She voiced out loud that she no longer had a reason to live. My brother and I were left trying to make sense of what had happened.

My parents were in and out of alcohol treatment centers. I was trying to care for them and for my brother Tim. With the hopes of starting over, my parents moved my younger brother to Alabama where they were planning on moving.But my mom began drinking again and decided to divorce my dad. Tim and I were now separated. I stayed home my first year of college to take care of my mom.

Within a year, my mom married another alcoholic. He moved into the home I had grown up in. I felt displaced and lost.

I applied to the University of Michigan, was accepted, and moved to Ann Arbor in 1981, not knowing a soul. When I arrived in Ann Arbor, I was very guarded and mistrustful. I felt I had been abandoned by my parents and that there was no one I could trust.

During my second semester I met some women who were part of a Christian group on campus called UCO. I was a mess, but I was so moved by their unconditional love. I began to get a glimpse of the love of God. Slowly the walls I had built to protect myself began to crumble.

In the fall of 1982, I went on a UCO retreat, and by God's grace I offered my life to Jesus Christ. I knew that becoming a Christian does not mean that my life will be easy or free of heartbreak or dis-appointment. My brother Tim and I had remained very close. After high school he joined the army and by God's grace he, too, became a Christian. We had both grown up playing guitar, singing and writing music. Now our music had a focus—the love of God.

My mom divorced her second husband and God began working in her life. She was struggling with alcohol addiction but trying to follow Jesus. My dad had moved to Alabama to be with family.

I became engaged in the fall of 1986 and my heart began to hope that all could be well, and I would live happily ever after. But there were storms raging below the calm surface and one of them was about to erupt.

One night in early December my mom was drinking and tried to cross a busy road in a snowstorm. She was hit by a car and killed. It was less than two months before my wedding.

Our first son was born in 1988 and our second son in 1991. I experienced significant post-partum depression after our second son was born. I was also seeing a counselor to help me deal with the losses of my past. It was a very dark season and I clung to God, though I couldn't see Him or hear Him. But after a year or so, God began to lift me out of depression and grounded me in His word in a deeper way than I had ever experienced before. His word became my rock. In His mercy, God was giving me a foundation on which I could stand through the fiercest storms.

My younger brother had moved to Ann Arbor to be near me. He was a Christian and an alcoholic. He struggled with the unresolved pain in his life and drinking was a way for him to keep the pain in check.

He was also my music partner. We wrote, performed and dreamed of recording our music which was in high demand.

In March of 1995, Tim was crossing a busy road in Ann Arbor and was hit by a car. He died six months later. I felt like my heart had been wrenched from my body. I couldn't get my mind around it. How could God let me lose another person? I had the naïve belief that after all the pain that I had gone through, God wouldn't take Tim from me, but then Tim died. God had grounded me. By His grace I trusted Him, though my heart was broken.

The day after Tim's funeral, I found out I was pregnant. It was difficult to understand God's timing and purposes during this time. I was grieving, we had just moved into a new home, and my husband was traveling a lot. Though God protected me from depression, it was a long, hard season in my life, full of tears and grief. And it's okay to grieve; it's good to grieve. We don't grieve as those without hope, but we grieve. God really does know best. That spring as the flowers began to bloom and the sun began to shine, and Easter drew near, our son Tim was born, and what a joy he has been.

I still grieved for my brother Tim; for all I had hoped for, all I had dreamed of. God began to show me that I wasn't going to be able to do what Tim and I might have done together, but God still had plans for me. I began to write and sing again—at church, weddings, funerals and ministry events. I still had the dream of recording, but the idea seemed overwhelming and the obstacles seemed huge—who did I know, how could we afford it, where would I find the time.

But once again, God had the answers. He provided an amazing producer and musician who worked with me in 2002. My first CD, "One Thing I Know" was released later that year and dedicated to my brother Tim. After a sold-out concert at The Ark in Ann Arbor, I began to get requests to share my story and my speaking ministry began.

In 2011, we were connected to a young woman in another state who was trying to escape her life of abuse and trafficking. God, in his amazing power, rescued her. I was recording my second CD, "Uncaged Bird", as God uncaged our beautiful new daughter.

Bruised and broken in every way—mind, body, and spirit, God has slowly healed our Melissa and made her a strong and healthy woman of God. She has touched many lives. We officially adopted Melissa in 2016 at the age of 38. She is now a paralegal and an elite runner.

Our older two sons have married, and all three sons are following Jesus wholeheartedly. I believe that we all dream of a happily-ever-after. As little girls we are drawn to fairy tales and happy endings, rescues and ransoms, princes and princesses and castles and kingdoms.

But life has a way of wounding and bruising our hearts, of disillusioning us and causing us to toughen up, and to let go of our dreams! In many ways, life can teach us that it's not safe to count on anyone; that we can only depend on ourselves. But the truth is, we are not alone. We belong to our heavenly Father. We are His, and nothing can separate us from His love for us. We are not orphans. We are not left to our own devices, needing to scrape along and provide for ourselves. We are living directed lives. God our Father oversees every detail of our lives and nothing comes to us that does not pass through His loving hands.

Life is full of both heartache and joy, loss and incredible gifts. There is no "happily ever after" in this life. We sin, others sin, we experience heartbreak and disappointment, people get sick and die. Life doesn't follow our well-laid plans.

But that's not the only truth. The Book of Revelation says that one day: "God will be with us and be our

God. And God will wipe away every tear from our eyes; there will be no more death, nor sorrow, nor crying. There will be no more pain, for the former things will have passed away and God will make all things new."

That will be our happily ever after. Until then, we live in this beautiful, messy world. But we are held, we are loved by an incredible God who has all things under His control for His glory and our good.

You see, God has been using all my life, all my circumstances, to change me and shape me and make me into who He created me to be. He did this not despite my losses and pain and grief but, through them. I can trust Him.

We all have stories. Deep stories of pain and loss and heartbreak; of joy and successes and dreams. And we need to know one another's stories. We can encourage one another. Things might look bad and things might feel bad. But we can trust that God is good all the time and He will work things out for our good and for His glory.

Questions to Ponder

How have you seen God's faithfulness in your own life during times of great pain or loss?

Do you believe that God can use anything and everything to make you into the person He created you to be?

How has God used pain or loss in your own life to bless others or draw you closer to Him?

God wants us to cling to Him whether we are experiencing joy or great pain. Our happy ever after will be in heaven, but God wants us to find "joy in the journey." In what ways do you look to your circumstances to make you happy, rather than finding joy in Christ, your life?

Author
Deb Mantel
Singer/Songwriter/Speaker/Professional
Organizer/Web Designer
Chelsea, Michigan

"After women, flowers are the loveliest thing God has given the world."

Christian Dior

Enjoy these publications by Dorothy K. Ederer

The Colors of the Spirit
A Golfer's Day with the Master
A Golfer's Prayer Book
The Spirit Whispers
Whispers from the Spirit
Spiritual Nourishment
Children Whisper to God
Nourish Your Soul
Love Stories
Spirituality of a Quilter
Jesus the Master Quilter
Wisdom for Life's Journey
Time with the Divine
Seasons of Love
52 Weeks of Inspiration
Dorothy and Dominic's Daily Devotional
Reach for the Stars
Fetty's Philosophy
24 Remarkable Women
The Divine Florist
Transformation
Reflections on the Prayer of St. Francis
Threads of Wisdom - A Daily Devotional
Advent - We Wait and Anticipate

Children's Books

Co-Created with Christopher Tremblay

Jesus' Alphabet
Joshua's Kids
A Message from God's Creatures
The Gift of Trees
Lucy's Laptop
The Wonderful Weather of God
Musical Instruments Believe
Going Places in Life
Here's the Scoop—the History of Ice Cream

Mandala Books

Follow Your Heart
Live Your Dream
Believe in Yourself
The Power of Mercy
The Gift of Hope
Praying the Psalms
Music for the Soul

dorteder.com